MOMS ON CALL

Next Steps Baby Care:
6-15 Months

Laura Hunter, LPN and
Jennifer Walker, RN, BSN

Moms on Call – Next Steps Baby Care: 6-15 months
Copyright © 2006 Moms on Call LLC All Rights Reserved
Revised 02/2016
Printing 3

Printed in the United States of America
ISBN **978-0-9854114-0-4**

Editing by Tim Walker
Photos by Alice Park Photography
Cover design and logo design by Kristen Smith and Alice Park
Family photo on back cover by Alice Park Photography

Published in the United States by
Moms on Call, LLC
5200 Dallas Hwy Ste 200 #226
Powder Springs, GA 30127

About the Authors

(Left to right -Jennifer Walker RN BSN and Laura Hunter LPN)

Laura Hunter (LPN)

Laura is a mother of five, pediatric nurse with over 20 years of experience, an entrepreneur and a highly sought after infant care consultant who has an international following. But there is one common passion for all the areas of Laura's life, her desire to inspire and encourage parents.

Jennifer Walker (RN BSN)

Jennifer has multiple roles—wife, mother of three, pediatric nurse, public speaker and infant and toddler care consultant. Jennifer has over twenty years of pediatric nursing experience and has a heart to equip parents with practical advice and inspiration for the joys and challenges of parenthood.

Moms on Call LLC is an Atlanta-based phenomenon. We started serving local families with in-home parenting consultations from birth to 4 years of age. And now, by combining technology, common sense and a passion for families, we have supported and partnered with parents all over the globe. Our books, swaddling blankets, online resources and seminars are all available at www.momsoncall.com.

"This book is dedicated to the living God who guides our paths and makes every day an exciting adventure."
- Jennifer and Laura

Seeking medical care whenever you are concerned is recommended by Moms on Call.

Any time that you are concerned, or notice any symptoms, call your pediatrician's office. Sometimes babies have discreet symptoms like a fever, and other times there is just something that you can't explain; call it mother's intuition or a nagging feeling that something may be wrong. Those are both valid reasons to seek medical attention. Many of the concepts addressed in this book vary from pediatrician to pediatrician. When it comes to your child's care, you are responsible for making the final decisions.

TESTIMONIALS

"Thank you for this book! It was the most helpful book that we received."
—Susan C.

"It is all about becoming educated as a new parent to build that foundation to raise great kids while keeping your home life intact. I plan to use Moms on Call for whatever needs arise."
—Liz H.

"I think that we were scared to do the 'just let her cry it out' thing, but it really wasn't that bad, and it took just a few nights. Thank you, thank you! Please feel free to use us as an example of parents who were 'parenting by accident' and then followed your instructions and discovered the joy of a system that works."
—Beatrice L.

"I joke that I'm entering my child into a sleep contest. He sleeps 11-12 hours at night and will take long two to three hour naps in the afternoon. A little genetics might contribute to that, I think, but also a lot of "moms on call"!"
—Jacyln A.

"What you say to do is what we thought was the right thing, but you gave us additional confidence to stand firm. Thanks!"
—Christine Q.

"You had given my husband and I advice about putting our 11-month-old to sleep. Everything you said would

happen did, and within two weeks she was sleeping soundly throughout the night. It has now been almost six months of our little girl sleeping through the night and we have you to thank."
—Jennifer R.

"I love those moms on call gals! So helpful, knowledgeable, and inspirational. Seriously!!! Moms On Call"
---T. Aycock

"I can't say it enough. Our lives have changed now for the better. Lyon is an incredible sleeper and through the pain/hell of sleep training, I realized that teaching my son how to soothe himself to sleep was one of the first lessons in life I would teach him. Witnessing him learn to fall asleep on his own was like watching my baby climb Mt. Everest! Truly miraculous and such a proud moment for us."
--- A. Parks

"I realize we all have had clients overseas. My family in the UK have been so supportive of us! However, just so you know, I have clients in REMOTE Northwest China and Kuala Lumpur, Malaysia currently. How exciting! Skype is wonderful!!!!!"
--Megan Tucker, RN, BSN (successful infant and toddler care consultant trained in the Moms on Call Nurse Training Program)

Table of Contents

Hello! We are Laura Hunter LPN and Jennifer Walker RN BSN, two moms and pediatric nurses who decided it was time to write a how-to childcare book that moms could really use—a book by moms and for moms that addressed reality. No psychobabble, not the exhaustive book of disorders that could cause immediate anxiety in the calmest of mothers. No—something different. Something we knew moms needed.

How did we know? Well, between us, we are raising 8 children: two girls (thank you Laura), two sets of twin boys and two singleton boys. We did so without nannies or night-nurses. Now, the clincher here is what we did to help earn enough money to be home during the day to enjoy each and every sloppy meal and stay home at night to snuggle up to whichever child had the current virus that was going around the school.

As we mentioned, we are pediatric nurses. Not only pediatric nurses, but nurses on call. When the busy 9,000-patient pediatric office was closed and moms had questions after hours, they paged us. So from 5 p.m. to 8:30 a.m. every weekday and all weekend, the pager went off. Every worry and need that any mom was experiencing about her child, be it medical or otherwise . . . we answered.

After about the 300th call about basic infant care, Laura decided she had to do something better to help teach these new moms how to care for their infants. So, she decided to do in-home infant care consultations. We developed a packet of information and instructions for new parents. Then, Laura went into parents' homes and went over the materials that we developed, helping parents to get their babies to sleep, and educating them on common infant care issues. After the first consult, we

11

knew that this is what God had purposed in our hearts. Testimonial after testimonial from pleased parents came pouring in. Every consult we did resulted in success story after success story and with no marketing at all, Moms on Call grew 600% over the first three years.

So, here we are as the result of the popular demand for the real story. Together, we developed this need-to-know manual that shares the realities of parenting.

Laura and I have answered thousands of questions from moms. We know what moms worry about at 9 a.m. We know what moms worry about at 4 p.m. We know what moms worry about at 8 p.m. and we definitely know what moms worry about at 2 in the morning. We know because it was our job to answer questions for many years, and we know because we have our own children. We have thought some of the same thoughts, and we have felt some of the same feelings. We know what moms worry about because we are moms.

There is a common fear of doing the wrong thing or making the wrong choice. When a baby is born, it is like a new part of your heart blossomed that you never knew was even there. This concept is impossible to explain; it can only be felt. We have been there. I (Jennifer) was so nervous with baby #1 (Grayson) that it was all I could do to leave him in the care of his incredibly capable and loving grandmother.

So, we have felt the sting of leaving baby #1 to go to work. That first day is a heartbreaker, and we suffered through it. By the time both of our twins came along, working outside the home was no longer a feasible option. Taking calls from home was a great compromise. Difficult, yes, but it has allowed us to interact with other moms in a way only another mom can, with a heart of compassion and understanding.

We did *not* do everything "right" with all our kids. We learned along the way, just like everyone else. We learned about the reality of parenting. And we, too, read the popular baby books. We got particularly frustrated when the advice assumed that there was only one child in the household, or that parents only have to deal with one child at a time. Most of the books left us feeling overwhelmed. It seemed as if they promised some instant fix that never came. So, if you are looking for a false sense of perfection, you will not find it here. What you will hopefully find here is a succinct, easy-to-read reference guide.

Children are amazing and wonderful creatures, full of mysteries and wonder. We desire to use our experience and education to help you enjoy the treasure or treasures that God has so graciously given you. He thought you were the best parent for this child/children. You may not have a degree or even a good role model, but He chose you. We want to help equip you with some of the information that we know moms need. This book will not make you a perfect parent, but perhaps we can help you enjoy the ride.

SECTION ONE: THE BASICS

What Every Parent Needs To Know
About Basic Baby And Early Toddler
Care

*"Keep sound wisdom and discretion; so they will be
life to your soul and grace to your neck."*
Proverbs 3:21b-22

GENERAL SHOPPING LIST

Moms on Call recommends having the following items "on hand" prior to needing them. This will cut down on any middle of the night trips to the pharmacy after you speak to the pediatrician's office.

These items are the ones that we have in our own closets. So, if you want to know what two pediatric nurses with eight kids keep in the medicine cabinet, this is it! These items can be found at www.momsoncall.com.

> **Note:** Do not administer any medications to your baby without consulting your pediatrician.

MEDICINE CABINET

- o Liquid Acetaminophen - (2-3 bottles)
- o Acetaminophen Suppositories
- o Children's Ibuprofen for use in babies over 6 months of age (2-3 bottles)
- o Diphenhydramine Liquid (2-3 bottles)
- o Normal saline nose drops (plain saline)
- o Glycerin suppositories
- o Pedialyte® (electrolyte replenisher)
- o Pedialyte® popsicles
- o Digital Thermometer (2-3)
- o Vaseline®
- o Medicine dosage syringes
- o Infant gas drops

DIAPER RASH ITEMS

- Vitamin A&D Ointment® (without zinc oxide)
- Lotrimin AF® (may find in foot care section of the pharmacy)
- Cocoa Butter cream
- Aqua-Phor Healing Ointment®
- Regular kitchen corn starch
- *Kirkland Diaper Wipes®*

SKIN CARE

- Aveeno Oatmeal Bath Packets®
- Eucerin® or Lubriderm® lotion

FIRST AID KIT

- Hydrocortisone 0.5% cream
- Hydrogen peroxide (2-3 smaller bottles)
- Polysporin Antibiotic Ointment®
- Anti-bacterial hand wash
- 4x4 Gauze - individually packed - (2-3 boxes)
- 2x2 Gauze individually packed - (2-3 boxes)
- Band-Aids® (flexible fabric)
- Ace bandages (2-3 rolls)
- Squeezable ice packs
- Tweezers (diagonal head) (2-3)
- Medical tape

MISC.

- o Baby pear or white grape juice
- o Canned peaches in heavy syrup
- o Bug repellent (Spray on hands, then apply to child sparingly, or just put repellent on baby's clothes and socks and a squirt on the stroller/carseat prior to placing baby in it.)
- o Sunscreen (Our favorites come in a stick for ease of facial application.)
- o Nail clippers by Safety First® (with the white handgrip)
- o Long handled infant spoons (usually one piece of plastic)
- o Biz laundry soap (Great for stain removal - especially if items are soaked overnight then washed in a regular laundry cycle.)

Note: Remember to always keep a digital thermometer, a bottle of Acetaminophen and a bottle of Children's Diphenhydramine secured in your diaper bag.

GROCERY LIST

These are just suggestions. This is not an exhaustive list of food choices. The Moms on Call Baby Food Introduction Calendar is a free download available at www.momsoncall.com.

*IMPORTANT - The following offerings must come in one of the following forms:
- o   Baby Food
- o   Puree at home
- o   Fresh; if it is pea-sized, soft, and mushable
- o   Canned; if it is pea-sized, soft, mushable and no extra sugar or salt added
- o   Frozen; if it is pea-sized, soft, and mushable

Fruit*
- o   Pears
- o   Apples
- o   Mango
- o   Banana
- o   Blueberries
- o   Kiwi
- o   Peaches
- o   Mixed fruit cocktail (make sure the grapes are smaller than pea-sized and mushy)

Vegetables*
- o   Spinach
- o   Kale
- o   Cauliflower
- o   Peas
- o   Green beans
- o   Broccoli
- o   Avocado
- o   Squash/Zucchini
- o   Butternut Squash
- o   Sweet Potatoes

- Carrots
- Cucumbers
- Corn

Grains and Legumes*
- Rice
- Oatmeal
- Whole Wheat Bread
- Cream of Wheat
- Cream of Rice
- Hummus
- Grits
- Beans
- Pasta
- Cherrios
- Veggie puffs

Proteins*
- Ham
- Chicken
- Turkey
- Chopped or roast beef
- White fish
- Eggs

Milk Products* (full fat content)
- Yogurt (Greek or no-added sugar)
- Soft Cheese
- Whole Organic Milk (introduce at 11 months)
- Ice Cream
- Whipped Cream

Sauces (For 12 months and older)
- Ranch Dressing
- Mustard
- Ketchup
- Italian Dressing
- Blue Cheese Dressing

FOOD ALLERGIES

Due to the ever-changing nature of food allergens, please check with your pediatrician regularly for additional guidelines.

Should your child have an allergic reaction to food, here is what you can do. Any facial hives are a reason to give Diphenhydramine and to seek medical care immediately.

Common reactions: If you notice the following symptoms, monitor closely, call the pediatrician and avoid suspect food for at least 2 weeks.
- Mild splotchy pink areas on face only
- Diarrhea and/or vomiting
- Itchy skin areas, exacerbates eczema

Severe reactions: If you notice the following symptoms, call **911!**
- Sudden difficulty breathing and/or swallowing
- Wheezing
- Tightness in chest or throat
- Excessive drooling
- Facial swelling
- Hive-like splotchy rash all over (together with any of the above symptoms)

Always keep Diphenhydramine (Benadryl) on hand. May need to see an allergist if food allergies are suspected.

BATHING

"When do I put my baby into the bath chair?"

Once your baby is sitting up on his/her own and can stay upright without assistance, you can begin to give the baby a bath in a baby bath chair.

You must <u>never</u> leave a child unattended in the bath. Babies can drown in less than two inches of water. However, as long as you do NOT leave them unattended, you can fill the bathtub with 5-6 inches of WARM water.

Always make sure that all supplies are kept within arm's reach. A basket of items is an easy way to ensure that everything is kept together.

- Towels
- Washcloths
- Baby soap
- Soft baby brush

Do not forget to wash the baby's genital areas <u>prior</u> to the bath with diaper wipes. Always rinse your baby well. Remember, giving a baby a bath every night as a part of the nighttime routine helps babies settle into the long stretch of relaxing nighttime sleep.

Females:
- Do not wash female genital areas with soap. Tip: Spread the labia (lip-like parts) and clean with a

diaper wipe or washcloth when taking diaper off PRIOR to bath. Always wipe FRONT to BACK so as not to introduce any stool into the urethra where the urine comes out. This will help us avoid bladder infections.

Males:
- o Circumcised: Prior to the bath when you are at the changing table, gently pull skin back so the entire head of the penis is seen, and clean well. Sometimes some diaper cream or stool gets between the skin folds around the circumcised area so this will help us to keep it clean.
- o Uncircumcised: Clean foreskin well. There is no need to retract the skin. Speak with your doctor for specific care.

BOWEL MOVEMENTS

"My baby is eight months old and I just introduced some finger foods. Now, she only stools once every three to four days."

Can you believe how we obsess over our baby's bowel movements? Color, consistency, frequency and amount of apparent straining are common concerns for moms. Let us set your mind at ease. There is a wide range of what is considered normal for a bowel movement.

Once the baby begins to have baby foods or finger foods, they may slow down to one bowel movement a day or even one a week! (If you are not lucky, your twins have simultaneous and copious stools eight times a day each until they are three years old. That's sixteen poopy diapers per day between them! - Jennifer) Now, let's carry on.

Color
- o   Breastfed: generally yellow seedy; can vary from yellowish brown to green
- o   Formula fed: darker in color; can vary from yellow to brown to green

Frequency
- o   Breastfed or formula fed: May vary greatly.
- o   They may stool as frequently as every feeding or as infrequently as once a week. What a difference!

> **Note:** The color of stools will vary from feeding to feeding, generally according to what the baby's body is absorbing and/or excreting.

Call pediatrician's office if:
- o More than 1 teaspoon bright red blood at any time
- o Less than 1 teaspoon bright red blood for 3 or more stools
- o Black tarry stools
- o What looks like coffee grounds
- o Clay (gray or beige) colored stool for more than 2 weeks

CONSTIPATION

True constipation is a term used to describe hard, pebble-like stools. There is a difference between constipation and infrequent stooling. Infrequent stoolers are gassy and have a large, **soft** bowel movement every 3-7 days.

Signs of Constipation
- Painful passage of stools when the stool itself is hard and pebble-like
- Abdomen is distended but remains relatively soft
- Decreased appetite

Relief measures if your pediatrician diagnoses constipation:
- Babies more than 4 months old (on baby foods) may have baby food, such as apricots, prunes, peaches, pears, plums, beans, peas, or spinach at least 2 times per day. Avoid carrots, squash, rice, and bananas for 3-4 days.
- Babies over 1 year old may have fruits and vegetables at least 3 times/day, pureed with peels. **Avoid any food your child cannot chew easily.** Increase fiber and offer plenty of water. Avoid cooked carrots, rice, and bananas for 3-4 days.
- In babies, you may stimulate a bowel movement with a rectal thermometer or Q-tip with Vaseline®. Insert ¼ inch into the rectum and

rotate Q-Tip® a few times. Rectal stimulation can be used every other day only if uncomfortable. If you have to do this for longer than 2 weeks, consult your pediatrician.
- o Glycerin suppository OTC (over the counter). If you have to use these for longer than 2 weeks, consult your pediatrician.
- o Your pediatrician can recommend a stool softener to be taken for approximately a week.

When to seek medical care
- o No relief after trying above
- o Abdominal tenderness (baby cries) when pressing on either side of the abdomen at the level of the belly button (Make sure your hands are not too cold!)
- o If fever over 101.5 F (rectally) is present
- o Happens frequently
- o Persistent vomiting (See vomiting section)

INFREQUENT STOOLERS

Signs
- o Soft stools: can be every other day to once every 7 days! That is a wide range for what is considered normal.
- o May have increased gas and/or fussiness

Relief measures for infrequent stoolers: (Only if the baby seems uncomfortable and with the approval of your pediatrician):
- o Rectal stimulation every other day only if uncomfortable. If you have to do this for longer than 2 weeks, consult your pediatrician.
- o We can add an ounce of juice in the morning and an optional ounce in the afternoon with the approval of the pediatrician to help produce stools. (Use Gerber pear or white grape juice by mouth in a bottle for up to 3-4 days)
- o Infant gas drops

Note: Infrequent stooling is not a problem and does not have to be treated. It is perfectly normal for many babies and toddlers.

NAIL CLIPPING

"I can't get my child's finger nails clipped. She keeps moving around so much."

Trim nails after a bath, when the nails are soft. This may take two people. You may also try to do this when the child is asleep.

- Trim <u>toenails</u> straight across to prevent ingrown toenails. You will not need to cut toenails as often as fingernails.
- When cutting <u>fingernails</u>, round off corners.
- As the child reaches 12-18 months, begin to "name" the different fingers. Children like this game. As they begin to talk, ask them to name each finger as you are clipping them. (The sillier the names, the better!)

Tip: Use nail clippers that have a white handgrip, pictured at <u>www.momsoncall.com</u>.

SKIN CARE

"My nine-month-old has a splotchy pink rash on her chin. It seems to get worse if she has been drooling all day."

It is very seldom that you see a child with perfect skin. Expect skin rashes. The pediatrician may diagnose your baby with one of these common skin rashes.

TYPES OF COMMON SKIN RASHES

Drool Rash: Pink splotchy area on the chin or cheeks that comes and goes. Can be caused by spitting up, pacifiers that hold drool against skin, or frequent drooling.

- o Rinse baby's face with water after feedings.
- o Apply Vaseline® to area to protect skin from irritation.

Heat rash: Pin-prickly pink bumps and splotchy areas. Can be seen on skin that touches mom's skin during breastfeeding or along the back where baby sweats in the car seat.

- o Change your baby's position during feeding.
- o Apply regular kitchen cornstarch (not baby powder) by putting cornstarch in your hand first, and then applying to affected areas. Be careful not to get the powder or the dispenser near the baby's face, as infants can choke on the powder.

31

Dry flaky skin: May use Eucerin® or Lubriderm® to moisturize skin. Dry patches may occur behind knees and elbows, although it may also appear in other areas such as the diaper area, or face.

Wet moist areas: Under neck, in skin folds. You may use cornstarch to help absorb the moisture that causes this redness.

Diaper rash

- **Redness.** Leave open to air (for as long as is practical!). May use diaper cream (Vitamin A&D®, Aquaphor®, Cocoa Butter). Apply kitchen cornstarch to keep moisture from irritating the skin. Change diapers frequently.

- **Red and bumpy.** Leave open to air (again, for as long as is practical). Change frequently. Apply Lotrimin AF® three times a day if approved by your pediatrician. Follow with any diaper cream listed above and kitchen cornstarch. Use for 7 days. If there is bleeding or no improvement in 3-4 days, then see your pediatrician.

Tip: Laura likes to use a combination of Aqua-Phor® and Cocoa Butter mixed together, then apply cornstarch. We also recommend Kirkland Diaper Wipes® (at Costco). You can also buy these in bulk, which is good because you will use more than you think.

ORAL CARE/TEETHING

"My child is so fussy. I am wondering if she is teething or has an ear infection?"

There is no way to definitively tell whether or not your baby has an ear infection unless the doctor looks in the ear.
Teething can begin as early as 2-3 months or as late as one year old. (Jennifer- My children had no teeth until they were about 11 months old. They discovered the joy of gumming everything from Cheerios to cheese!) Some children do not have any discernable irritation while teething. We all hope for that kind of child!

Signs
- o Increased drooling
- o Chewing constantly
- o Swollen, red gums

Relief Measures
- o Wet an infant washcloth slightly and put it in the freezer for 10 minutes. Allow them to chew on it as needed – supervised, of course.
- o Place a saline-filled teether in the fridge for 10-20 minutes and then let them chew on it.

> **Note:** It is very difficult to tell the difference between teething and ear pain. If running a fever more than 2-3 days, not sleeping well, grabbing at ears or has cold symptoms, call your pediatrician.

Dental Care once teeth erupt

- Usually the teeth break through in the following order:
  - 2 lower incisors
  - 4 upper incisors
  - 2 lower incisors and all 4 first molars
  - 4 canines
  - 4 second molars
- Begin brushing teeth/gums with wet gauze or washcloth wrapped around your index finger. Be careful not to let the gauze slip off your finger.
- You may use toddler toothpaste (fluoride-free) when the molars erupt. (Make sure it is fluoride-free.)
- When you begin using toothpaste, only use a pea-sized amount. Use toothpaste intended for infants/toddlers that can be swallowed.
- We want to encourage them to spit it out, but they will always swallow some of it.
- You need to supervise your child as they brush their teeth until they are around 6 years old.
- Begin flossing when the molars start to touch each other.
- Never allow your child to go to sleep with milk/formula residue on their gums/teeth. This causes painful tooth decay. **That means no bottles or sippy cups in the crib!**

The first visit to the dentist should be around 2-3 years old, but it can be earlier if there is noticeable tooth decay or problems, including chipped teeth. We recommend a pediatric dentist because they know how to deal with the unique problems that can arise for kids. Be aware that most pediatric dentists will have you sit in the waiting room while your child is treated. Your child will tolerate procedures much better without you (trust us!). Moms often are so anxious that it makes it difficult to calm the child.

CRYING

It is okay to allow your baby to cry 15-20 minutes at a time. We do not want your baby to have more than 2 hours of inconsolable crying during the day and we are not asking you to ignore their basic needs, such as diaper changes and feedings. Just be prepared for babies to cry for no apparent reason in the evenings and 15-20 minute segments during the day. It does not necessarily mean that you are doing something wrong. When toddlers do not get their way, or another child snatches their toy, they cry. It is a natural expression of the normal frustrations of life. Here are some common reasons your child will cry.

Behavior-related
- o Generally begins around 12-15 months old. They begin to exert their free will.
- o In response to not getting their way or hearing the word "no" for any reason
- o Under 12-15 months, it is best to try to distract the child with another activity.

Over-stimulation
- o A 6-15 month old cannot handle the hustle and bustle of the adult lifestyle. Make sure that *all* the naps are not in the car or "on the run" - as much as reality allows.
- o Be aware of your child's limitations.
- o Allow time for quiet play.

Normal Frustrations
- o Children learn by practicing. They do the same

thing over and over again. It may take 20-30 times of doing something the right way and/or the wrong way before they consistently do it the right way. Continue to allow them the opportunity to learn.

o If your child is about to crawl and is crying for a toy across the room, do not get it for him/her/them. Their frustration level can motivate them to achieve developmental milestones.

o Allow the baby a moderate level of frustration and crying. Monitor and encourage them as they try to crawl, walk, and learn to soothe themselves to sleep. Allow them to have a few minutes of cry time as that frustration is quite normal.

o They do not know how to share—allow them a few toys that are only theirs.

o If siblings are fighting over a toy, take the toy away.

o **It is okay for an early toddler to be frustrated. But it is not OK to hurt others or emotionally hijack the entire household.**

o If they lash out, hitting the mommy or another child then they go straight to "simmer time" in a child-proofed place with light and space. They get a good 5-10 minutes to let that frustration out where they cannot hurt anyone. After 5-10 minutes, we give them a hug and tell them "you do not hurt others". If this is happening frequently, then it is time for the Moms on Call Toddler Book!

o For the expanded behavioral guidelines see book 3, The Moms on Call Toddler Book.

FRUSTRATION

Babies cry.

They will do so much less if they are on a predictable routine and sleeping well at night. These things will help reduce frustration for everyone. The "Typical Days" and the "Sleep" sections of this book will provide step-by-step guidelines that aid in establishing a household that has **significantly reduced frustration levels** *by design.*

Here are a few things to remember
- o   Your child's behavior is not an indication of your self worth. You are valuable no matter how they behave.
- o   Everyone else does NOT have it all together.
- o   Your child is strong, resilient and adaptable and so are you. You are not going to ruin them.
- o   You are going to run late.
- o   You are going to make mistakes.
- o   You are going to be OK.
- o   We believe in you.

TWINS

"My twins are eight-months-old and still do not sleep at night. We are exhausted!"

Here are the survival tactics that helped us:

1. **If one baby eats, they both eat--period**. Even if one twin does not appear hungry, feed that one anyway. Keep them on the exact same schedule and we mean it! It is okay to put them both in bouncy seats and feed them simultaneously with bottles. Just remember to talk softly to both of them and give them each a few minutes of your full attention. Breast-feeders can hold both babies in the football hold and feed at the same time.

(Jennifer- I did not like the way simultaneous breastfeeding felt and decided to breastfeed one baby and bottle feed the other on an alternating basis. At each feeding, whomever bottle fed last time became the breast feeder and the other one got the bottle. I would breastfeed the one baby in the cradle hold while holding a bottle in the other baby's mouth with my "free" hand. The baby with the bottle was generally propped up on a nearby bouncy seat or Boppy® pillow. This way they both were getting at least half of their nutrition from breast milk every day. And they were fed, burped and changed in 45 minutes!)

It is also good to allow Dad to feed the babies sometimes. He can feed both with pumped breast milk or formula from a bottle. It gives Dad a chance to have that much needed interaction.

2. **When one baby sleeps, the other does also. Naptimes and bedtimes are the same.** (See #4 for specific guidelines for "Bedtime.") Again, one baby may not seem sleepy at the same time as the other. This is survival mode. They will learn to be on the same schedule. This is part of learning to live in a family environment. One twin may have to learn to sleep more to accommodate the family schedule. Exception: If one baby wakes 15 minutes earlier from a nap, it is fine to get that baby up a little early.

3. **Use your helpers**. In the first two or three years (honestly), you will be absolutely exhausted. If grandma comes for a visit one day, allow her to watch the babies while you nap for an hour or two. If neighbors or friends ask how they can help, allow them to make a meal or arrange for household chores. Many people would love to help if they just had a tangible thing to do. Let others make meals for you. If someone you trust offers to babysit, say "That sounds great; when are you available?" Think of it this way: the more you allow others to help, the more time you will have to actually enjoy your twins!

4. **Use the Moms on Call Method of getting your babies to sleep.** We do realize that some moms do not have the extra hands around at night. Also, single parents of twins are more likely to have to do the "Bath time" and "Bed time" routines alone. So, here is a way to do the "Bath time" and "Bed time" routines if you are alone.
   o   Put both babies in the bouncy seat in the bathroom.

- Transfer them both into the tub seats and you can have them play together in the tub as you wash and play with them.
- When you are done, transfer each one out into the awaiting bouncy seat with a towel in it. Once they are both bathed and both sitting in their towels in the bouncy seats, then...
- Take them one at a time to their room (you can place them on a towel or blanket on the floor or in the crib.) Go get the bouncy seats and put them in their room.
- Dress them in their pajamas one at a time.
- Put the first baby back in the bouncy seat (buckled) momentarily while you dress the other baby.
- So, when they are both dressed and back in the bouncy seats in the nursery, play soft music; feed them their last nighttime feeding (don't forget to burp them).
- Place them in the crib; turn on the white noise and turn off the lights.
- The babies can sleep in the same crib or separate cribs. They can even have their own room, if you have the space.

Letting them cry takes on new meaning with multiples. However, we have often found that one twin can wake and scream while the other sleeps as if nothing is happening, so do not assume that the crying child will wake the sleeping child. When you have a firm nighttime routine, even if the sleeping child awakens, they can both learn to soothe themselves back to sleep if given three to five nights of consistency. I know that you do not want the 'good sleeper' to have to suffer, but his/her help is

41

needed in teaching the other twin that screaming does not get you an automatic "get out of crib free" card. Three nights, three nights, three nights. It works! (Laura – I child-proofed the twins' room and when I put them to bed, I closed the door and let them cry it out for three nights. And let me tell you, they put on a show of tears and banging on the door, but I persevered. Now they are wonderful sleepers.)

5. **Remember, it gets easier as they get older.** Twins are incredibly labor intensive for the first three years. Double the work, but double the love! The great news is that they will hit a period of time when they are continuous playmates. It is easier to have two 18 month olds, because you are not their only source of entertainment. They will play together and keep each other amused for years. It is wonderful. (Jennifer – My mom is a twin and she described it this way: "Having a twin is not like having another brother or sister, it's like having another you.")

SECTION TWO: COMMON ILLNESSES

A Quick Reference Guide To Common Illnesses For This Age Group

"The glory of the LORD shall be your rear guard."
Isaiah 58:8

COMMON ILLNESSES

"I am not sure if this fussiness is teething or an ear infection."

Here are some general descriptions of illnesses that are usually seen between 6-15 months. The following pages are for reference only. These pages are not to be used for diagnostic purposes. Only qualified medical professionals are able to accurately diagnose and treat an illness.

The illnesses that will be described in the following pages are:
Fever
Common Colds
Coughing
Hand-Foot and Mouth Disease
Roseola
Croup
Falls
Lacerations
Otitis Media (Ear Infections)
Vomiting
Diarrhea
Reactive Airway Disease/Bronchitis

We also wanted to share with you a list of general symptoms that require immediate medical care. This list includes but may not be limited to:
   o   Seizure activity
   o   Unresponsiveness

- Inconsolable crying for 2 or more hours
- Abdominal pain that hurts worse (doubled over) if you press one inch to the right or left of the bellybutton.
- A bright red or purple pin-prickly rash that does not blanch to white when you apply pressure with your finger. This rash is noticeable and sometimes almost looks like freckles. In a child who is lethargic and has a fever, this is one sign of meningitis. Other signs include: headache, neck stiffness (ask if your child can put his chin to his chest) and lethargy.
- Hive-like rash all over with facial swelling around the lips and eyes that has a sudden onset.
- Any difficulty breathing – if you are concerned that your child is unable to get air in and out of their lungs, you should be at the ER. Difficulty breathing can be accompanied by the following symptoms:
  - Ribs becoming pronounced on inhalations.
  - Squeaky noise on exhalations.
  - Breathing faster than 60 times per minute. (Place your hand on the child's chest and count how many times the chest rises in one full minute.)
  - Coarse noise when inhaling (stridor) that sounds like a gasp or squeak with each breath.
  - Lips are blue or purple.
  - Cannot stop coughing long enough to breathe.

FEVER

"My 14-month-old has a fever of 103 rectally."

We get so many calls about fever. This is a misunderstood symptom. Our bodies are designed to fight off infection. One way that the body does that is to turn up the heat when a virus or bacteria is detected, hoping the bacteria or virus will not want to stick around if it gets too hot. So, mild fevers in babies **over 3 months old** can be quite beneficial.

It is also imperative that you are able to take an accurate temperature. When taking the baby's temperature, we recommend taking rectal temperatures exclusively until the baby is over 18 months old. That is the most accurate way to take a temperature. The ear thermometers, forehead thermometers and pacifier thermometers are just not as accurate in infants.

In babies over three months old, normal rectal temperatures are between 97-100.5 degrees Fahrenheit. In babies over 3 months old, we would not consider their temperature a "fever" unless it was over 100.5°F rectally.

Temperatures may vary according to several factors, including activity level and times of day.

Taking a Rectal Temperature (see a demo at www.momsoncall.com)

1. Lubricate the thermometer with a pea-sized amount of Vaseline®.
2. Lay infant on back as if changing a diaper.
3. Lift legs so rectum is easily seen.
4. Press button on thermometer to turn it on.
5. Insert thermometer into rectum about ¼ inch or until you can no longer see the silver tip of the thermometer.
6. Hold thermometer in place 3 minutes or until it beeps -most digital thermometers only take about one minute before they beep
7. Remove and read thermometer

Daytime Treatment
- o **If over 6 months old**, if irritable or fussy and/or not resting well, may use Acetaminophen or Ibuprofen as directed by the pediatrician.
- o Give extra fluids.
- o Fevers generally subside during the day and spike in the late afternoon. No need to treat a fever under 102.5°F rectally unless the child is uncomfortable.
- o Treat the child, not the numbers on the thermometer. We are much more worried about a child that has a mild fever but is lethargic (like a wet noodle all day) than we are a child with a 104°F rectal temperature who is running around like nothing is wrong.

Nighttime Treatment
- o Put child in the crib or toddler bed wearing cool cotton clothing. No fleece zip-ups or warm

blankets. Temperature of the home should be between 68-72 degrees.

o   If he/she wakes up and feels very hot, undress the child down to the diaper/underwear and give whatever fever control medicine is due next. Avoid taking their temperature for ten minutes. (The temperature will spike right when the child awakens. If we give the child about 10 minutes of being undressed, the fever will generally come down 1-2 degrees all by itself. This helps us to avoid a big parental breakdown over a 105°F rectal temp.)

o   There is normally a wait at the ER and by the time you have given a child fever control medicine and arrived at the ER, the fever is under control. However, high fevers that are accompanied by other symptoms may need to be evaluated such as but not limited to:

    o   Neck stiffness

    o   Bright red or purple rash that does not blanch or lighten with pressure

    o   Persistent vomiting (more than twice)

    o   Severe abdominal pain

    o   Inconsolable crying greater than one hour

    o   Difficulty breathing (not increased breathing; respirations will be increased when they have a fever.)

    o   Severe headache

    o   Seizure activity – violent shaking

When to seek medical care

o   If more than 6 months old, if the temperature >103.5°F rectally, call your pediatrician

o   A baby with any temperature that is lethargic

(like a wet noodle) all day. Any child that is not having at least 20-30 minute periods of playfulness at any temperature can be a sign of illness.

o Fever accompanied by other symptoms such as, but not limited to: a rash, vomiting, decreased movement of a limb, difficulty breathing, inconsolable crying longer than an hour or an abdomen that is hard like a table when the baby is at rest

Febrile seizures: These are generally harmless and are a result of the fever going up too fast, not the fever getting too high. These may last 1-3 minutes. Usually febrile seizures begin at 6 months to 2 years old, with the first seizure occurring by the time the child is 2 years old. They normally stop by the time the child is 5-6 years old. Febrile seizures generally will occur in the first 24 hours of fever. Only a pediatrician or emergency room doctor can adequately diagnose this type of seizure.

Treatment
o Keep area safe.
o Do not try to restrain your child. Once started, it will run its course no matter what you do.
o Once the seizure is over and your child is awake, give usual dose of medicine if due. (Acetaminophen® or Ibuprofen)
o Do not over-dress your child. When the seizure has subsided, holding the child too close to your body can also cause the child to get overheated, so be careful with the cuddling at this time.

When to seek medical care:
- o This is the first febrile seizure
- o Lasts longer than 3 minutes
- o Neck stiffness
- o Confused or delirious
- o Difficulty awakening
- o Any seizure activity in absence of a fever

Note: Acetaminophen and Ibuprofen do not cure the cause of the fever. It is for comfort only. Once these medications wear off, the fever will come back until they are no longer sick. Often the child's temperature will not come all the way back down to normal. It can hover between 101°F-102°F rectally in an infant over 3 months even with fever control medicines.

EYE DRAINAGE

There are many reasons that a baby can experience eye discharge. Generally, eye drainage is not an emergency. However, it is best to contact your pediatrician if there are any related symptoms, such as the ones described below.

When to seek medical care:
- o Thick yellow or green discharge that reappears after wiping away several times a day
- o Eye redness or swelling (especially swelling that goes up to the eyebrow, or below the eye approximately one inch or lower.)
- o Symptoms appeared immediately after a possible foreign body entered the eye (The sand box is a great place to get a scratched cornea.)
- o Complaints of pain/ frequent rubbing
- o Fever

Eye Discharge: Can be viral, allergy related or bacterial.

Viral
  Signs
  - o Eye redness on the inner lids and/or white part of eye (sclera)
  - o Watery discharge or thick mucus discharge from eyes. (Usually occurs with a cold and it can produce crustiness in the a.m.)

  Treatment
  - o Wipe away any mucus with a warm, not hot, washcloth while eyes are closed

When to seek medical care
- o   No improvement of symptoms in 2-3 days
- o   Eye redness or swelling, especially swelling that goes up to the eyebrow or below the eye approximately one inch or lower
- o   Fever
- o   Ear pain
- o   Sensitivity to light

Bacterial Eye Infections
Signs
- o   Yellow-green discharge from eyes that has to be wiped away every 20-30 minutes
- o   Usually will have pinkness or redness to white part of the eye (sclera)
- o   Puffiness to eyelids
- o   It can also produce crustiness in the a.m. but the mucus keeps reoccurring every 20-30 minutes, even when awake.

Treatment
- o   Antibiotic eye drops (have to be prescribed by the pediatrician)
- o   Warm compresses with a clean, warm (not hot) washcloth

When to seek medical care
- o   No improvement in symptoms after using antibiotic drops for 2 days
- o   Showing signs of an ear infection (See section on ear infections.)
- o   Fever -- Ask your pediatrician for a fever handout.

- Swelling of the eyelids that goes up to the eyebrow or down to the area where we usually get dark circles under our eyes when we do not get enough sleep

Allergies – Eye
Signs
- Itchy eyes with frequent rubbing
- Increased tearing (<u>clear and watery</u>)
- Pinkness or redness to the white part of the eye (sclera)
- No pain or fever
- Seems to occur around the same season or around the same allergen (dog, cat, outdoor play area, etc.)

Treatment
- Diphenhydramine or OTC antihistamine by mouth with pediatrician's approval
- OTC allergy eye drops (has to be recommended by your pediatrician according to child's age)

When to seek medical care
- No improvement of symptoms in 2-3 days
- Swelling that goes up to the eyebrow or below eye approximately one inch or lower
- Fever
- Ear pain
- Extreme sensitivity to light

Note: Always remember to wash your hands frequently.

COMMON COLDS

It is quite common for babies over 6 months old to have nasal congestion. We even have a term for it, amazingly called . . . the common cold. Babies who are in daycare, church nursery or play-group can expect to have between 4-8 viral colds between October and February. It makes for quite the healthy immune system (so, no guilt working mommas!).

Colds
Signs (may have some but not all of these signs)
- o Runny nose
- o Nasal congestion
- o Possible fever, generally under 103.5°F rectally
- o Sore throat (usually determined by decrease in appetite)
- o Cough with **no difficulty breathing**
- o Watery eyes

Relief measures if approved by your pediatrician:
- o Use non-medicated saline nose drops. Instill 2-3 drops in each nostril. You can use the drops 5-6 times a day. It breaks up the thicker congestion. Saline is not harmful to the eyes or mouth so if you miss that little nostril, it will be fine.
- o After you instill the non-medicated saline drops, if they still seem congested; you can use the bulb syringe to suck out the mucus. Only use the bulb syringe 3-4 times per day or it will become an irritant. Use bulb syringe to suck the saline out of

the nostrils. Depress bulb, hold one nostril closed, insert tip in open nostril. At the same time, slowly remove the bulb syringe while releasing the suction of the bulb and doing a sweeping motion in nostril. Use preferably before a meal and before bed. You can see a video example at www.momsoncall.com

o   Temperature in home: winter 68-70 degrees; summer 72-74 degrees

o   Dress the baby as you would dress yourself, as far as layering and seasonal appropriateness. If you are wearing long pants and a long sleeve shirt, then baby should be in long baby pants and a long sleeve baby shirt. May use a short-sleeve Onesie® underneath.

o   May use a cool mist humidifier.

o   Elevate head of bed. Do not place any objects **in** the child's bed or crib. You can use a rolled up towel UNDER the mattress to tilt it.

o   If the nose is very runny and the baby is not resting well, check with your pediatrician.

o   You may clean the outer lids of eyes with a warm washcloth several times a day.

o   If the child has fever, see Fever section of this book. Be careful when using multi-symptom products. Some products already contain Acetaminophen -listed on the "active ingredients". Therefore, it is not advisable to give Acetaminophen (typically known as Tylenol®) in addition to a multi-symptom cold medicine that already contains Acetaminophen.

o   Increase fluids. The child may not want to eat as they often swallow a bunch of mucus down the back of their throat. This makes them lose their appetite (understandably!)

o Generally with runny noses, it bothers us more than it bothers them.

When to seek medical care
o Frequent cough with no improvement after doing above (Frequent=several times/hour)
o Chest sinking in when breathing or ribs pronounced during inhalations
o Nostrils flaring
o Wheezing (whistle or squeaking sound)
o Stridor noise made on inhale when not coughing; tight sounding
o Breathing faster than 60 respirations/minute
o Call pediatrician if temperature is more than 102.5° F rectally
o Symptoms last longer than 10 days.
o Pulling on ears and/or not sleeping well for 2-3 nights
o Worsening sore throat or copious (freakishly large amount) drooling.

Note: Colds are not curable. Comfort measures are used to help with symptoms. No medicine approved in children will make the cold go away any faster. There are hundreds of different cold viruses, and most healthy children will get 6-10 colds/year. Careful and frequent hand washing, frequent wiping of nasal drainage, and helping your child learn to cough into the crook of their elbow can help manage the transmission of these viruses. We recommend keeping baby wipes in several rooms of the house and washing down everyone's hands several times a day.

COUGH

The nagging nighttime cough is the source of much parental stress. As soon as there is a change in the weather, kids begin to get stuffy noses, nasal congestion and a post-nasal-drip (PND) cough that has mucus and gets more frequent at night. Unfortunately, at this time there is not a medication, prescription, or otherwise that will get rid of the PND cough.

Signs
- A productive (bringing up mucus) cough that often gets worse when activity is increased or the child is in a horizontal position.

Treatment
- Cool mist humidifier in the room at night, especially if you are running the heat in the house
- Nasal saline: 1-2 drops in each nostril (use the nasal syringe to suck out the mucus only about 3 times per day immediately after the saline).

When to seek medical care
- Fever over 102.5° F rectally
- Your child has a history of Reactive Airway Disease or asthma, or your child ever needed an inhaler or breathing treatment in the past
- Lethargic all day (like a wet noodle)
- Any signs of difficulty breathing, such as:
  - Ribs getting pronounced on inhalations

- Squeaky noise on exhalations
- Breathing faster than 60 times per minute (Place your hand on the child's chest and count how many times the chest rises in one full minute.)
- Coarse noise when inhaling (stridor) sounds like a gasp or squeak with each breath
- Lips are blue or purple
- Cannot stop coughing long enough to breathe

HAND, FOOT AND MOUTH DISEASE

Hand, Foot and Mouth Disease (a.k.a. Coxsackie Virus) can last 7-10 days, with most of the discomfort caused by the mouth sores, which tend to be gone by days 4-7.

Signs
- Small blisters in mouth or down the throat
- Sometimes the baby may have small bumps on the hands, feet or genitals that look like they are pus-filled, but you cannot pop them or get any pus out of them
- Fever
- Sore throat

Treatment
- Miracle Mouthwash (with your pediatrician's approval): Liquid Diphenhydramine, Liquid Mylanta® (or equivalent store brand that has your pediatrician's approval), and liquid Ibuprofen mixed together in the same medicine cup and given every 6 hours according to the appropriate dosage for your child's weight for each medicine
- Popsicles, cold drinks, milkshakes, and Jell-O® are soothing to the throat
- Avoid citrus, salty or spicy foods

When to seek medical care
- Fever for more than 3 days

- Signs of dehydration (not urinating for 6 hours; inside of bottom lip is dry when you swipe your finger along the inside of the lip, no tears when crying, lethargic)

Note: This illness is very contagious. It may take 3-6 days for other children to develop symptoms after exposure. Because it is generally harmless, children can typically return to daycare after they are 24 hours fever-free.

ROSEOLA

Roseola is a viral illness characterized by three nights of high fevers (generally 103°F-104°F rectally) and then a fine pink rash appears on the torso and face as the virus leaves the system. Once the rash appears, the child is no longer running a fever and is no longer contagious. Other children can develop symptoms within 12 days after being exposed.

Signs
- o Usually happens between 6 months old and 3 years old
- o Fever: Usually over 103°F rectally for 3 nights *followed* (on day 3 or 4) by a pink pin-prickly mildly raised rash on the torso and face
- o Once the rash appears, there is no more fever and the child generally feels much better
- o Rash lasts 1-2 days

Treatment
- o Monitor child - treat fever while present

When to seek medical care
- o Fever for more than 3 days
- o Rash that looks purple or scarlet red and does not blanch (whiten) when you apply pressure to it
- o Child is lethargic even when the fever control medicine has kicked in (Fever control meds usually 'kick in' in about 20-40 minutes.)
- o Rash lasts more than 3 days

CROUP

Croup is common in children from 1-5 years old. It is generally caused by a virus, which irritates the upper airway and vocal cords. Swelling of the vocal cords causes hoarseness and can also narrow the passage in the upper airway, making it difficult for your child to breathe. This illness generally lasts 3-4 nights with the second night being the worst. It is commonly better, if not gone, during the day. The worst symptoms are generally seen in children under 3 years old.

Signs
- o Harsh, strong, barky cough (often described as a "seal barking"); Onset in late afternoon, early evening
- o Temperature 100°F-101°F rectally- although it can go higher
- o Hoarse cry and/or voice

In severe croup, you may notice the following symptoms that would require immediate medical intervention:

Signs of severe croup
- o A harsh, raspy or squeaky noise made when inhaling
- o Labored breathing - ribs pronounced during inhale
- o More than 60 respirations/minute

o   In the beginning these symptoms happen only when crying or coughing, and then progresses to happening even at rest

Treatment- If you feel your child has croup, call your pediatrician. He/she may recommend some of these relief measures:

o   Go to the smallest bathroom in the house and run a hot shower so the bathroom steams up nicely. DO NOT PUT THE CHILD IN THE HOT SHOWER. Sit in the bathroom with the child so they can breathe in the warm steam, which is very soothing to the airways. Read a story or cuddle with your child; because the more relaxed they are, the faster they can recover from the coughing spasms.

o   Immediately after the 10 minutes of steam, open the freezer and let the child breathe in a blast of cold air or open the door and take the child outside for a few seconds if it is below 65 degrees.

o   Run a cool mist humidifier in the bedroom during this illness; it helps to have moist air.

o   Warm, clear fluids may help relax and loosen the sticky mucus on the vocal cords.

o   If they are running a fever, you may treat them with Acetaminophen or Ibuprofen if that is acceptable with your pediatrician.

o   Do not let anyone smoke around your child or inside your home . . . EVER!!!!!

When to seek medical care (at ER if "after hours" or unable to see pediatrician at office immediately):

o   If above measures fail to improve stridor (squeaky noise made on inhale)

- If excessive drooling or difficulty swallowing
- If chest is sinking in around ribs during inhale
- If nostrils are flaring
- If there is a fever more than 3 days or any fever >103.5° F rectally
- If the croup lasts longer than 3 nights or happens more frequently than once a month

Call 911 if:
- Stops breathing
- Lips or nail beds turn blue
- Child is unresponsive
- Increased difficulty breathing that worsens even after treatment

FALLS

All children fall at some point. When they are learning to walk and/or climb, these accidents generally begin. Most falls, in our experience, result in a bump on the forehead. Usually the swelling can cause a "goose egg." There is not much soft tissue on the forehead so it always looks big when swelling occurs.

Head injury with no lacerations:
- May apply ice packs to decrease swelling for 20 minutes if tolerated.
- Do not give any pain medications. If pain is severe, call your pediatrician.
- After your child goes to sleep the first time after a head injury, make sure they can be awakened every 30 minutes for 2 hours. Keep in mind what is normal for your child.
- Check pupils to make sure they get smaller when the child is exposed to bright light. Turn lights off and check pupils with a penlight. DO NOT USE A FLASHLIGHT. They are often too bright and can damage the baby's eyes.

When to seek medical care - Watch for these symptoms for 48 hours:
- Persistent vomiting (more than twice)
- Severe headache (early toddlers will often bang their head against the floor to try to alleviate a headache, so look for that sign in conjunction with these other symptoms)

65

- Pupils not reacting to light by getting smaller, or one pupil is large and the other small
- Marked sensitivity to light
- Difficulty awakening; seems confused
- Difficulty walking or talking
- Breathing abnormally
- Extreme moods: either an hour of inconsolable crying or marked lethargy
- Not urinating
- Not moving a limb or sensitive when a limb is moved or touched
- Abdominal pain - the baby cries out when you touch the abdomen (make sure your hands are not too cold)
- If the fall was from a distance greater than four feet, you suspect that the baby's neck got twisted, and/or the baby is not moving or crying: DO NOT MOVE THE BABY. Immediately call 911.

LACERATIONS

Clean well with soap and water. Apply pressure with a wet and preferably sterile 4X4 gauze pad for as long as it takes to stop the bleeding.

When to seek medical care:
- If wound edges are not touching or wound is gaping
- Bleeding does not stop with pressure within 5-10 minutes
- Bleeding is severe and/or pulsating out of the body
- Any laceration on the face

Note: You have a right to ask for a plastic surgeon to repair any facial lacerations if you so choose. However, the best way to access a plastic surgeon is through the local ER.

OTITIS MEDIA (EAR INFECTIONS)

Ear Infections/Otitis Media: Usually starts with a cold. The fluid that the cold produces becomes trapped behind the eardrum. Bacteria and viruses love to live in that warm, moist environment and begin to grow. Once the area has become infected with bacteria or a virus, more fluid collects behind the eardrum and causes pressure; babies generally experience discomfort. Over 80% of ear infections are viral. That means that antibiotics will not help the ear infection to get better. Time, patience, and comfort measures are the key. However, if your pediatrician prescribes antibiotics, then it is fine to administer them. The recent outbreaks of antibiotic resistant bacteria are secondary to the overuse of antibiotics; so allow the doctor to help you use discretion when treating any illnesses (ear infections included). Remember, ear infections may cause discomfort, but are typically not life threatening. (Laura has had to sit up with Blake many nights due to ear pain and pressure – no fun!)

Signs
- Ear pain—pulling at ear frequently
- Crying when laying flat
- Not sleeping well
- Fever for more than 2-3 days (although ear infections are frequently present without a fever)
- Cold symptoms

Treatment
- OTC May use Acetaminophen or Ibuprofen for pain control
- Allow them to sleep with the head of bed elevated.
- Cool mist humidifier in the room at night to help with the cold symptoms
- Saline nasal spray
- It is fine to let the sleep patterns get interrupted when your child has pain or illness. We can always be back on track in about three nights when they feel better.

When to seek medical care
- No improvement of above symptoms within 3-4 days

Note: Ear infections can occur in babies who have no symptoms at all. This is an impossible disorder to treat based on symptoms alone. Sometimes we will find ear infections in children who are being seen for a physical exam and have no symptoms. This is a difficult area for moms. The key is to watch your child for classic symptoms. In the absence of symptoms, there is no way to know when to take your child to the pediatrician. However, if your child is only pulling at the ear but is sleeping and eating well, then it is okay to wait a day or two before making an appointment.

VOMITING

"My kid just threw up and I don't know what to do."

Vomiting: large amounts of vomit, with forceful emptying of stomach contents, more than 2-3 times. Although there are various causes of vomiting, we see it most often associated with a gastrointestinal virus. These types of viruses usually start with vomiting every 30-45 minutes for the first 6-8 hours then maybe an isolated episode of vomiting on day two or three. Diarrhea will often accompany these symptoms and it lasts for 5-7 days. (See diarrhea section.)

Treatment:
o Try to wait about an hour after the child vomits.
o Then you can try one tsp of clear liquids (water, Pedialyte or breastmilk) every 10 minutes for the first 2-3 hours while awake, with an occasional teaspoon of heavy peach syrup (not to exceed two teaspoons of peach syrup in 24 hours. Now you know why we mentioned the peaches in heavy syrup in the general shopping list! It coats the stomach and helps the baby keep the liquids down.)
o You can then begin to increase the amount of clear liquids by adding another teaspoon of clear liquids every ten minutes for the next 2-3 hours. (One teaspoon, wait ten minutes, two teaspoons, wait ten minutes, three teaspoons and so on.) Sucking on popsicles or a wet washcloth is a way of ensuring that they are not swallowing too

70

much at one time. A teaspoon of Jell-O® would be good. You can sit on the couch and give sips of clear liquids from a medicine dropper if you need to as well.

o   If the child goes 6-8 hours without vomiting try to breastfeed a limited amount, increasing as tolerated or use 1-2 ounces of formula every 30 minutes for 2-3 hours as tolerated.

o   If no vomiting after 12 hours, begin returning to a normal diet slowly.

o   If the baby vomits during any of above, return to step one.

o   Avoid giving medicines for 8 hours (with the approval of the pediatrician). If running a fever of 102° F or more rectally, then use Acetaminophen suppositories if permitted by your pediatrician.

o   If older than a year, no milk for 24 hours from the last time that they vomit. After no vomiting for 6-8 hours try starchy foods such as toast or crackers and gradually return to a normal diet.

Common Errors
o   Giving too much fluid at one time.
o   Not waiting the hour before beginning fluids.

Sometimes when a gastrointestinal virus is causing vomiting in a child, no matter what you feed them or how often you feed them, the vomiting will continue. If your child is crying for fluids and it has not been an hour after vomiting, it is okay to give it, just try to have them drink slowly. (We realize that you only have so much control over how quickly they drink.) When they are experiencing these symptoms, it is crucial to monitor for the following additional symptoms.

When to seek medical care
    Signs of dehydration
- Not urinating at least every 6 hours (You may want to place toilet tissue in the diaper to check for wetness because the absorbent nature of today's diapers makes it hard to tell if the baby has urinated at all.)
- When you run your pinky finger over the inside of their bottom lip, it is dry and tacky as opposed to smooth and moist
- Tries to cry but cannot cry tears
- Marked lethargy
- Unable to hold down one tablespoon of fluid after 2-3 attempts (Remember to wait 30 minutes to an hour after each vomiting episode)
- Vomits blood
- Neck stiffness
- Rash
- Vomiting that continues > 24 hours
- Fever (see Fever section)
- Vomiting bile - fluorescent yellow or green goo
- Abdomen hard and tender at rest (hard like a table top, as opposed to soft like a really full balloon)
- Blood in stool (more than 1 tsp bright red blood)
- Call pediatrician if the child has a fever of 102.5° F rectally or higher

DIARRHEA

"My 9-month-old has had diarrhea that exploded out of the diaper 5 times today. I've had to change his clothes every time."

Diarrhea can be caused by a gastrointestinal virus and can generally last 5-7 days. However, sometimes babies may have a day of diarrhea secondary to mild stomach irritation, and this will pass in one or two days.

Signs:
- More than 5 watery stools in a 24-hour period.

Relief measures—We do not like to give medication that claims to stop diarrhea for infants or kids under 2 years old. This is because most diarrhea is caused by a gastrointestinal virus that will run its course. We want the diarrhea to get out of the baby's system. This is the body's natural way of handling this kind of virus.

Infants
- Formula Fed: Continue Formula feeding as usual
- Breast-Fed: Continue to breastfeed
- Baby food for babies > 4 months old: Baby foods that are starchy are good choices, i.e., cereal, applesauce, bananas, carrots, mashed potatoes.

Children greater than one year old:
- Water is the best fluid for your child with diarrhea, unless they are not eating well, then you may use Pedialyte®.

- After 24 hours, you may give milk as well as water
- AVOID fruit juices. Exception—if this is the only thing they will drink, you may give fruit juice to keep the baby hydrated.
- Solids--starchy baby foods (i.e., rice cereal, bread, crackers, rice, noodles, potatoes, carrots, applesauce, and bananas). Fatty foods are good as well.

Note: Regardless of how you feed diarrhea, it will generally run its course. However, it's probably not the time to get Mexican for dinner.

When to seek medical care
- 8 or more watery stools a day for 5 days.
- Blood or mucus in stool.
- Fever (see Fever section)
- Abdominal tenderness/hard at rest.
- **Any signs of dehydration:**
  - Longer than 6 hours without urinating
  - No tears when crying.
  - Inside of lips feel dry when you swipe your pinky finger along the inside of bottom lip
  - Increased lethargy

Note: Diarrhea is very contagious. All family members need to wash hands well after changing diapers and/or using the toilet.

REACTIVE AIRWAY DISEASE/ BRONCHITIS/BRONCHIOLITIS

"I have been giving my child the inhaler as directed and the cough is more frequent and he is bringing up more mucus when he coughs."

Upper respiratory viruses generally trigger the airways to swell and become more narrow. These airways are lined with mucus and when they narrow, it is hard for the child to dislodge the mucus. The prescription medication: Albuterol/Xopenex/Proventil will help open up the airway so the child can move air through the airways and dislodge the mucus.

What to expect: In the first 24 hours of treatment, the child will:
- o Get a more frequent, more productive sounding cough. The cough will slowly improve after the first 24-48 hours and should be markedly improved within 5 days of beginning treatment.
- o The child may seem like they have a rapid heartbeat and may be on the "hyper" side for the first night or two of treatment. This is the trade-off for being able to breathe and will subside in a day or two.
- o The child may have *isolated* (i.e., not persistent like every 30-45 minutes) episodes of vomiting (mucus triggers the gag reflex).

When to seek medical care: Sometimes the airways do not respond to the medications in a way that improves breathing. The signs that the symptoms are getting worse are:

- o Retractions: this is when the ribs get more pronounced when inhaling. You can almost count the ribs with each inhalation. This is an indication that the child is using accessory muscles to move the air in and out of the lungs. They are working too hard to get the air they need.
- o Respirations are faster than 60 times in one full minute. Put your hand on the child's chest and count how many times the chest rises in one full minute. (If you count more than 60, recheck in 3-4 minutes; if still above 60, seek medical care.) Normally, a baby or young child will breathe 20-30 times per minute.
- o Bluish or purplish hue around lips
- o Shortness of breath with moderate activity
- o Audible wheezing—this is a squeaky sound when exhaling as opposed to a rumbling or mucousy sound
- o Coughing so frequently that they cannot get air in between coughing fits
- o Mucousy sounding breathing, with every breath that is not cleared with a cough
- o Symptoms are unchanged after the first 24 hours of treatment

SECTION THREE: FEEDING

_____

_____

Feeding Without Fretting

"When wisdom enters your heart, and knowledge is pleasant to your soul, discretion will preserve you; understanding will keep you"
Proverbs 2:10-11

BABY FOODS AND SOLIDS

"When can I start baby foods? I need to know how much to feed my baby and how often to feed her."

Basics for beginners 4-6 months
You may begin baby food (Stage One) between 4-5 months of age. We really want these babies to have started baby food by 5 months of age at the latest, so that we do not miss the perfect developmental window. If you have not started, and your baby is 6 months of age; start today. Be prepared to wear a good deal of baby food over the next month.

For a super easy printable feeding guide, see "The Moms on Call Baby Food Introduction Calendar" free download at www.momsoncall.com

The most important thing is to have a low-stress, happy atmosphere, even if the baby seems to not like it at first.

- o HAVE FUN, giggle often, and take lots of pictures. We are simply getting them used to different tastes and textures.
- o RELAX, we want your face to indicate that this is normal and fun. They are watching you.
- o Babies get 100% of their nutritional needs met through the formula and breastmilk until 12 months of age, so we do not need to worry about amounts.

- Mix 1-2 tablespoons of baby cereal with formula or breastmilk until the consistency is almost like smooth yogurt.
- Use the long handled spoons and place the food on the tip of the spoon. Place the spoon in the baby's mouth and allow the spoon to sit in the baby's mouth while you hold the spoon.
- Always start new foods in the morning to see if it agrees with them.
- Order of introduction: Baby cereal first, then fruits and veggies (See "The Moms on Call Baby Food Introduction Calendar" free download at www.momsoncall.com)
- If it seems to upset them, (increasing fussiness and frequent spitting up), stop *that* food and wait 1-2 weeks to try that food again.
- Do not feed them out of the baby food jar; pour the food into another container and feed from there. The bacteria from their mouths (by way of the spoon) will contaminate the jar of food. Once opened, an uncontaminated jar should be refrigerated and used within 48 hours.
- Amounts are relative at this stage. The baby may take 1-2 spoons one day and 5-6 the next.
- REMEMBER, this is a gradual process however, not **too** gradual. Move from a thin, yogurty consistency to thicker consistency with some texture (a consistency like adult rice pudding) within a little over a month.
  - Stage one – very pureed x 2 weeks
  - Stage two – thicker pureed for 2 weeks
  - Stage three – thickest puree until they start mushable finger foods at 7 months
- **Vitamins/Supplements**
  Consult your physician at the baby's next

check-up to guide you in vitamin supplementation. Herbs and homeopathic remedies are usually not tested on infants and children under 6 years old. Therefore we cannot recommend any herbal preparation. That is not to say that they are harmful. There is just not enough information available about their safety when used in children or infants.

BABY FOOD INTRODUCTION SCHEDULE

Here is a basic rundown of how to introduce baby foods. Please visit www.momsoncall.com to download our free Moms on Call Baby Food Introduction Calendar for an easy-to-follow, printable guide that you can display on the fridge.

Days 1-3
- o Begin with 1-2 tablespoons of baby cereal mixed with formula or breastmilk until it is the consistency of yogurt. Give this in the morning and afternoon for three days.

Days 4-6
- o Now we add pears to the morning feeding. We can either mix it in with the baby cereal or we can give it separately.
- o Baby cereal WITH pears in the afternoon
- o We are gradually increasing the menu.

Days 7-9
- o Now we have the option of moving to three meals a day. (If you have multiple children and all you can do is two baby food feedings a day; that is fine.)
- o We can add squash to the morning feeding. We can mix the squash with baby cereal.
- o The mid-day feeding and/or the supper feeding is cereal, pears and squash (not necessarily mixed together)
- o A typical day can look like this:
  - o Baby cereal and pears or squash for breakfast

- Cereal, pears and squash for lunch
- Pears and squash for supper for three days.

Days 10-12
- Now we add apples to the morning feeding. We can mix it with the baby cereal or give separately.
- Then the rest of day we have the option to give pears & squash or apples & squash (not necessarily mixed together).
- From here it can be 3 meals a day, introducing a new food every three days and adding them to the above menu. Go back and forth between fruit and vegetables. We are looking for variety. Fruit will always taste better then vegetables no matter what order they come in.

Sippy Cups for 6 months
- You may begin putting small amounts of **formula/breastmilk** or water in a sippy cup (Starting the sippy cup with formula or breastmilk in it will increase the chances that the baby will want to take it).
- The baby/babies may only sip occasionally and it will take time for them to learn how to suck out of this type of cup.
- At mealtimes, place the tip of the sippy cup on the tongue and hold it there for a few minutes (or as long as reality allows).
- It is important to get babies used to the *presence* of the sippy cup at meals even if they do not drink from it for several months.

FEEDING 7-12 MONTHS

"When can I start giving my baby finger foods?"

Around 7 months, begin slowly with mushable finger foods. Remember, it will take time to master these skills. There should be finger foods available at every mealtime by 8 months of age.

- Begin to offer soft, mushable, pea-sized finger foods
- Only 2-3 pieces on the tray at a time!
- Let them play with it, touch it, squish it, explore it. They have never been able to explore food so it is new to them. They may even eat it.
- It is OK for mealtime to be messy.
- It is very important to move to increased texture. When we wait too long to introduce texture we miss our best developmental window and it can result in difficulty managing solids.

Finger Foods: pea-sized and mushable
- Cheerios (a few at a time)
- Soft, very tender, cooked diced baby carrots, green beans, potatoes
- Soft tender baby fruits: diced pears, mangos, peaches
- Scrambled egg (remember to watch for allergies), Be sure to cook thoroughly.
- Thin toast in small pieces, only a few pea-sized pieces at a time
- Small pea-sized pieces of soft cheese

- Gerber meat sticks, diced one at a time
- Soft pasta
- Avocado diced in pea-sized amounts
- Sweet potatoes (baked and diced)
- May puree foods you have prepared for your supper. Example: Casseroles--puree slightly or finely chop with a fork and knife. (Watch sodium content.)
- Amounts increase as tolerated but still show up on their tray, 2-3 bites at a time.
- The baby/babies should have at least 3 different food groups with each meal.
- Remember that babies have varying appetites. At one meal they may want 10 bites and at another meal only 3.
- The amounts are not important until the baby is 12 months old.
- It may take a child 10-15 times of trying a food and spitting it out before they actually swallow it.
- Variety, variety, variety. We just want to expose the babies to different tastes and textures.

Anything soft that you can dice into pea-sized pieces is generally acceptable with the exception of the following: whole nuts, honey, and shellfish. Always be aware of possible choking hazards. This is also a great time to refresh your CPR skills by taking a CPR class offered through the American Heart Association. It is a great idea to know what to do in the event that your baby has a choking episode.
Choking hazard foods include, but are not limited to: peanuts, raw carrots, pieces of apple, uncut grapes, popcorn, hotdogs sliced too large.

In addition, bread or bagels should only be given under close supervision.

Examples of serving sizes - Serving sizes are smaller than you expect. Remember, the baby's stomach is approximately the size of _their_ fist. All foods are pea-sized and mushable.

- ¼ medium-sized piece of diced fruit
- ¼ cup of diced fresh or canned fruit (Always get fruit that is canned in its own juice with no sugar added.)
- ¼ cup dried diced fruit
- ½ cup raw leafy vegetables, diced and soft
- ¼ cup (2 ounces) cooked or canned vegetables, diced
- ½ cup (4 oz) 100% low sodium vegetable juice
- ½ slice of soft, thin-sliced whole wheat bread in small pea-sized pieces; offer with liquids.

Sippy Cups

You should be putting small amounts of **formula/breastmilk** in a sippy cup around 4-6 months of age. If you have not started this and your baby is over 6 months of age, start today. The baby/babies may only sip occasionally and it will take time for them to learn how to suck out of this type of cup. What we are trying to establish is familiarity. We do not want the child at 12 months of age to have never seen a sippy cup in their life.

- Place the tip of the sippy cup on the tongue and hold it there for a few minutes (or as long as reality allows).
- You may offer the sippy cup frequently, even if they only want to play with it at first. It is

important to get babies used to the presence of the sippy cup at meals even if they do not drink from it for several months.

o Starting the sippy cup with formula or breastmilk in it will increase the chances that the baby will want to take it.

Formula/ Breastmilk amounts:

7-12 months old: 24-32 ounces/day (including milk used in cereal). Once you begin baby foods and solids, you may notice a decrease in the amount of overall formula or breastmilk, bringing the total closer to 24 ounces. If nursing exclusively, they may decrease time on the breast and/or go to 3-4 good nursing sessions per day. There is a normal decrease in appetite at 9 months of age.

<u>**Individual feeding amounts 7-12 months**</u>

<u>**Bottles**</u> will contain
 o 6-8 ounces of formula/breastmilk
<u>**Sippy cups**</u>
 o 4-6 ounces of formula or breastmilk when we replace the bottle for the morning feeding
 o 2-4 ounces of formula or breastmilk for other daytime meals and all snacks
 o Do not worry if they are not taking everything in the sippy cup. They are just getting used to it at this time.

SAMPLE MENUS 7-12 MONTHS

Each of the following choices are *"in addition to"* the regular breastfeeding or bottle feeding for babies under a year.

Breakfast choices: sippy cup of formula/breastmilk (2-4 ounces) is available plus, any of the following options:
- o Baby cereal: 1 ounce mixed with formula or breastmilk and ½ a jar of baby fruit (2 ounces)
- o Regular oatmeal or cream of wheat- (not thick, sticky or lumpy)
- o Scrambled eggs with cheese and thin-sliced ham bits
- o Grits with cheese and scrambled egg; small bites (not thick, sticky or lumpy)

Lunch Choices – sippy cup of formula/breastmilk (2-4 ounces) is available plus, any of the following options:

- o 2-4 ounces of vegetables (diced or baby food)
- o 2-4 ounces of fruit (diced or baby food)
- o 1-2 ounces of dairy (soft cheese or full-fat yogurt, ice cream)
- o 2-4 ounces low-sodium vegetable soup
- o 2-4 bites of a grilled cheese sandwich cut up in pea-sized amounts

Supper Choices - Sippy cup of formula/breastmilk (2-4 ounces) is available, plus any of the following options:

- 2-4 ounces of vegetables (diced or baby)
- 2-4 ounces of meat (diced or baby)
- 2 ounces of fruit (diced or baby)
- 1-2 ounces of bread or pasta or rice

Snack Choices – Sippy cup of 2-4 ounces of formula/breastmilk and any of the following options:

- Cheerios
- 1-2 ounces of fruit (diced or baby)
- soft cheese in pea-sized bits
- yogurt

Amounts of food are not critical. They will generally eat what they need, even though it seems to be such a small amount.

The child may not take all that is offered in the sippy cup every time the sippy cup is available. Do not force them to drink all of it.

FEEDING 12-15 MONTHS

"My baby is only drinking about 12-16 ounces of milk. He used to have so much more when he was on formula. Is this okay?"

12-15 months old: 12-16 ounces/day- Once a baby is 12 months old, their nutritional needs shift significantly. This is a huge change for **the parents**. The amount of breastmilk or formula prior to 12 months of age was such a huge focus and now it decreases. This is good and normal.

At 12 months:
- o **They only need to have between 3-4 servings of milk _OR_ milk products per day.**
- o Each serving size is between 3-4 ounces
- o For example: They could get 3-4 ounces (minimum) of whole milk in the morning and afternoon. Then have a serving of ice cream or yogurt at suppertime and be just fine.
- o Mealtime is fun and stress-free.
- o Mealtime is fun and stress-free.
- o Mealtime is fun and stress-free.
- o No, those were not typos!
- o We can begin to offer baby spoons and baby sporks (not the cheaper plastic kind). Let them play and figure out how to use it. It will be messy!
- o They can eat one bite or twenty bites.

- Your job is to provide the food. Their job is to eat it (sometimes they will not want to eat and that is ok!)
- Offer at least three different food groups with each meal.
- Their tummy is the size of their fist. Do not offer adult-sized portions.
- They have a 10-15 minute mealtime tolerance window before they are ready to get down.
- Throwing food is normal. They will outgrow this frustrating behavior.
- Offer variety. Do not stick to only what you know they will eat (unless you are having a super stressful day, then – by all means – just feed them what they will eat and move on)
- Turn the high chair so it is facing the table like everyone else.
- Let them watch you eat.
- Let them hear you talk about how good something tastes.
- Do not put all of the attention on them.
- We want to invite them into the land of independent feeders. (Do not sit face to face with the baby at every meal.) Keep it low key.
- They love to dip at this age so offering a muffin tray filled with different sauces will help you to find that "magic" ingredient that can be put on many items. (In my house, it is ranch dressing and it goes on all sorts of foods.)
- We prefer whole organic cow's milk for all children unless they have been diagnosed with milk sensitivity. Be sure not to use fat-free milks because the babies need the fat to develop vital organ systems!

SAMPLE MENUS 12-15 MONTHS

Offer the liquids first at each meal or snack. Mealtimes are pea-sized, mushable versions of what you are having plus a sippy cup of whole milk (avoid low-fat meals for toddlers- they need healthy fats). Here are some great options:

Breakfast Options
- o Sippy cup of 2-6 ounces of whole milk and one of the following:
- o One egg with cheese, ½ piece of toast and ½ piece of diced fruit
- o ½ cup of oatmeal ½ piece of toast and ½ piece of diced fruit
- o ½ cup of grits mixed with cheese, bacon or ham, ½ piece of diced fruit
- o ¼ cup of crushed Cheerios in 2-4 ounces of yogurt

Lunch Options
- o Sippy cup of 2-6 ounces of whole milk and one of the following:
- o ¼-½ cup of vegetable soup, ¼-½ grilled cheese sandwich, ½ piece of diced fruit
- o Small chicken/cheese quesadilla with sour cream, ½ piece of diced fruit
- o ¼-½ of chicken salad or egg salad sandwich, chicken diced pea-sized
- o ¼-½ cup of vegetables one ounce of soft cheese

Supper Options
- o Sippy cup of 2-6 ounces of whole milk and one of the following:
- o 2-4 ounces of vegetables
- o 2-4 ounces of soft meat
- o 2 ounces of fruit
- o 1-2 ounces of bread, pasta or rice

Morning/Afternoon snack options
- o Sippy cup of 2-4 ounces of whole milk and one of the following:
- o Dry cereal
- o Fruit
- o Cheese
- o Yogurt
- o Graham crackers

Keep a sippy cup of water available all day long. **There is no need for juice at this age**. (If you choose to give juice, use the 'no sugar added' variety. You can dilute juice greatly with one part juice, 3 or 4 parts water, if preferred.)

> **The child may not take all that is offered in the sippy cup every time the sippy cup is available. Do not force them to drink all of it.**

Early toddlers (just like babies) will generally eat what they need. Often it seems to be such a small amount. But they get what they need in the day when they have a variety of foods available at each meal. They may only seem to eat well at every fifth meal and that is the unpredictable and normal way of the early toddler.

Speak to your pediatrician if you are concerned about their growth or nutrition.

Feed a variety of nutrient dense foods and have fun at the dinner table. Do not allow meal time to escalate into a war of the wills over the chicken nuggets. We do not care if your child ever eats a chicken nugget. Just offer varieties and enjoy your food in front of your children.

Making good eaters is about controlling the atmosphere more than the food. This should be a low-stress, fun activity. Do not count bites. Let them explore. Let them have a varied appetite. Let them join you in a normal dining experience.

If mealtime has become a stress-filled mess, it is time for the Moms on Call Toddler book. If you are worried about weight gain, see your pediatrician.

WEANING

This can be a very emotional transition for moms. Here is a text exchange with a friend that you may find helpful.

Friend: I will not be able to breastfeed any longer; I am taking some medicine that will not allow it and I am heart-broken.

Response: My bottle-fed-as-a-baby son just chose to take me to our favorite college team's bowl game. We bonded. Not because I breastfed him, but because I loved him. You see, good moms have something in common: they feed their babies. That formula's nutrition is calculated down to the last milligram, but it's the hand that holds the bottle that has the magic. It's the heart of the mom who wants to do everything the best that makes the bond. That baby, the one that you hold and worry about and love- well, that baby is not missing one thing. That baby has everything any baby would hope for because that baby has you...and you, my friend are spectacular.

At Moms on Call, our motto is "Feed your baby." Good moms feed their babies. Breast, bottle, combo – all good choices – just feed them. That said, there are two ways to wean a baby <u>6-12 months old</u>.
- o One Feeding at a Time
- o Cold Turkey (Weaning a baby <u>over 12 months</u> old is best achieved by using the 'Cold Turkey' method.)

With either method it is best to:
- Relax! Sometimes the first few feedings are a fight, especially if mom is the one doing the feeding. They will get the hang of it.
- Feedings should take 10-20 minutes, but no longer than 20 minutes, and they should be able to get between 6-8 ounces in that time.
- Under 12 months of age –**THIS WILL SAVE YOU SO MUCH HASSLE** -Use either the Gerber FIRST ESSENTIALS medium flow nipples on 9 ounce bottles or another **old-fashioned, standard-looking nipple** (in our vast experience, breast-shaped nipples will not be helpful).
- Do not switch formulas every few days—pick one kind and stick with it.
- If you are weaning after 12 months of age, then go straight to a sippy cup with organic whole milk (soy or milk alternative can be used for those with a milk sensitivity).
- Stay on a very clear schedule so that feeding times are predictable. Use the schedules provided in this book (in the "Typical Days" chapter) according to the age of your baby.
- It is normal to grieve that last breastfeeding. Give yourself some time to shed some tears, and then choose to look forward to the upcoming feeding methods that you will continue to enjoy with your baby.

Formula Basics
- Expect 5-7 days of fussiness, gassiness, and changes in bowel habits. This is normal.
- Between 24-32 ounces of formula a day is generally sufficient for healthy babies between 6-12 months old.

- Never reuse formula (or breastmilk) left over in a bottle for over an hour, whether it was refrigerated or not.

Types of Formulas: When using formula, always follow the directions on the can.

Powder
- Least expensive.
- May be prepared ahead of time or 'on the go.'
- Only use water to mix with formula. You can store it in the refrigerator for up to 48 hours. Using tap water ensures the baby is getting some fluoride. In some areas boiling tap water is necessary. If you are on well water, boil your tap water for 5 minutes and then let cool.

Concentrated:
- Use equal amounts of tap water and formula.
- This mixture of formula may also be stored in the refrigerator for up to 48 hours.

Ready to feed:
- Most expensive. May use occasionally, but remember that ready-to-feed formulas do not contain any fluoride.

Changing formulas:
- Do not change formulas without checking with your doctor.
- If formula is changed:
  - It will take the child several days to adjust to a new formula.
  - Stools will change, they may increase or decrease and can vary from firm to loose.

o   Increased gassiness/fussiness

Temperature for feedings:
   o   You may try different temperatures (from cool to warm) to find which your infant prefers. Typically, they do not like it straight out of the refrigerator. If warming, place the bottle in a cup of warm water and ALWAYS CHECK TEMPERATURE BEFORE FEEDING.
   o   Never use a microwave to heat bottles. Microwaves heat unevenly and what you test on your wrist may feel fine, but portions of formula in the bottle can be scalding!

Amounts
   o   Babies 6-12 months should be getting 24-32 ounces of formula per day.
   o   There is a normal decrease in appetite for babies around 9 months of age.

'One Feeding at a Time' Method -6-12 months
With this method, we switch one breastfeeding to a bottle every 3-5 days.

   o   Our goal is to use their 24-hour clock to know what time the bottle-feeding is coming. If we try the same feeding TIME each day, they learn faster. Which means, you can pick the 11am feeding each day to introduce the bottle.
   o   If we are trying bottles at all different times with all different people, nipples, methods, temperatures, etc., then they take longer to sort all that out.
   o   Start with one mid-day feeding. Replace the same mid-day feeding with a bottle for 3 days.

97

o   Basically, at that feeding time, the baby has 20 minutes to get as much as they can get out of that bottle. Your job is to hold the bottle in position, and their job is to fight, spit and act like they hate it for 20 minutes. Then we are done, and they do not eat again until the next scheduled feeding time. This only lasts about 3-4 attempts/days, and then they get the hang of it.

o   After 3-5 days, replace the second mid-day feeding with a bottle. This will go easier.

o   Then you are left with morning and evening breastfeeds. You can stay here as long as you would like, but if you are ready to continue weaning, then after 3-5 days you can drop the next breastfeeding.

o   Then you are left with one breastfeeding per day.

o   After 3-5 days (or whenever you are ready), switch the final breastfeeding with a bottle.

Cold Turkey Method <u>6-12 months</u>

o   Replace each feeding with a bottle filled with 6-8 oz. of formula. Start with the morning feeding.

o   Use the schedules listed in the "typical days" section of this book. At each breast/bottle feeding listed, use only the bottle.

o   Basically, at that feeding time, the baby has **20 minutes** to get as much as they can get out of that bottle. Your job is to hold the bottle in position and their job is to fight, spit and act like they hate it for 20 minutes. Then we are done and they do not eat again until the next scheduled feeding time (this only lasts about 3-4 attempts/days and then they get the hang of it).

o   The baby has a maximum of **20 minutes** at each

time listed in the schedule to finish what they can get in that time. If they only eat 2-3 ounces, then they will have another 20-minute opportunity to feed at the next scheduled bottle-feeding.

- o Some babies take to it right away and get 6-8 ounces in 10 minutes or under. That's great. In that case, we are done until the next scheduled feeding time.
- o If, after 3 days, they continue to take less than 4 ounces in a bottle-feeding, switch to the next level of nipple flow. We want to get 24 ounces per day, minimum. If we do not reach that goal by day 3-5 of this process, then contact your pediatrician.
- o It takes about three days of replacing each breastfeeding with a bottle-feeding before they become accustomed to the new familiar. They may seem like they hate it, but they do not hate it, and they do **not** hate you. This is just unfamiliar.
- o For mom: wear a very tight sports bra continuously for about 3-4 days.

Cold Turkey Method <u>Over 12 months of age</u>

- o Early Toddlers between 12-15 months should be getting between 12-16 ounces of organic whole milk per day **OR** 3-4 servings of milk products.
- o We go straight to a sippy cup – no need to do bottles at this age.
- o Brands of Sippy Cup: you can use whichever one you like. Just pick one and stick with it. If you are just starting this process: the first few times have the plastic spill-proof stopper out of the cap to

help the milk come out faster.

- o If you have not introduced a sippy cup at all: use a sippy cup with 4-6 ounces of organic whole milk. At each time listed in the "Typical Days" schedules, spend about 5 minutes trying to 'help them' with the sippy cup (holding it for them, tipping it up).
- o After 3-5 days of 'helping them', just have it available and do not worry if they are not interested in it. Also, have it available at breakfast, lunch and dinner when they are eating solids.
- o We prefer organic whole milk. We only recommend organic milk alternatives like soy or almond for children with a diagnosed milk allergy. Both options are full fat, not reduced fat.
- o When we go cold turkey, we completely discontinue breast-feedings and bottle-feedings (once they have 5 minutes of time being exposed to the sippy cup that first morning, we move on). Do not breastfeed them afterwards. Do not turn back; it will only confuse them.
- o They may seem like they hate it, but they do not hate it, and they do **not** hate you. This is just unfamiliar.
- o It takes about three days before they become accustomed to the new familiar.
- o They often take what they need from the sippy cup when THEY are thirsty. Once you have spent 2-3 days giving them a few 5-minute opportunities to see how this works, your job changes. Then you relax and just have a sippy cup available throughout the day.
- o Your child can do this. They adjust much better when the sippy cup is the only option, and you

are as relaxed as possible at feeding times.
- o Give it three days, but if you are ever afraid that they are dehydrated or they are not urinating 3-4 times a day, then contact your pediatrician for additional assistance.
- o The best thing you can give them is time, consistency and confidence. Keep your face as relaxed as possible. You've got this.

The child may not take all that is offered in the sippy cup every time the sippy cup is available. Do not force them to drink all of it.

TRANSITION TO SIPPY CUP

By following these gradual guidelines, we can make the transition much smoother and be ready for the independent feeding stage at 12 months of age (the babies will not even realize what happened, and we are well on our way to building great feeding habits).

How to introduce a sippy cup:
- o Brands of Sippy Cup- you can use whichever one you like. Just pick one and stick with it.
- o If you are using a brand that has a spill-proof element; then the first few times you introduce it, have the plastic spill-proof stopper out of the cap to help the flow come out faster.
- o Use the age appropriate schedules listed in the "Typical Days" section of this book to determine when to offer the sippy cup.
- o At each time listed in the "Typical Days" schedules spend about 5 minutes trying to 'help them' with the sippy cup (holding it for them, tipping it up). After 3-5 days of 'helping them', just have it available and do not worry if they are not interested in it.
- o We prefer organic whole milk. We only recommend organic milk alternatives like soy or almond for children with a diagnosed milk allergy. Both options are full fat, not reduced fat.

> **The child may not take all that is offered in the sippy cup every time the sippy cup is available. Do not force them to drink all of it.**

6-7 months
- o Sippy cup has 2-4 ounces of formula or breastmilk and is present while we feed baby food. Do not force it. The biggest thing we want to establish is **familiarity** with the presence of a sippy cup.

8-10 months
- o Sippy cup has 2-4 ounces of formula or breastmilk and is now offered at the newly introduced snack times.
- o Keep in mind that babies have a very normal decrease in appetite at 9 months of age.

11 months
- o Sippy Cup – still offered at snack and mealtimes.
- o A week before the first birthday, we will gradually replace bottles of formula/breastmilk with whole milk in a sippy cup.

One week prior to the 1st birthday
If you want to continue to breastfeed past 12 months of age, please do. The following is for families that are planning to transition to whole milk at 12 months.

Bottle fed
- o We are going to gradually introduce whole milk (or milk alternative for those with sensitivities). They will not take as much out of a sippy cup as they did out of a bottle. That is normal.
- o At this time, the nutritional needs change, and we are no longer dependent on liquids as a source of primary nutrition.

- Morning and evening of day one: sippy cup has 3 ounces of formula/breastmilk and 1 ounce of whole milk.
- Morning and evening of day two: sippy cup has 2 ounces of formula/breastmilk and 2 ounces of whole milk.
- Morning and evening of day three: sippy cup has 1 ounce of formula/breastmilk and 3 ounces of whole milk.
- Day four –all whole milk.

Breastfed – see below

Cold Turkey method 12-15 months

- At this age, we go straight to a sippy cup.
- Great news! Early Toddlers only need between 12-16 ounces of organic whole milk per day **OR** 3-4 servings of milk products per day. Read that again.
- We want you to have confidence that your child can do this.
- If you have not started a sippy cup yet, remember:
    - Brands of Sippy Cup- you can use whichever one you like. Just pick one and stick with it.
    - Use the sippy cup at each time that you previously did a bottle or breastfeeding. If you are just starting this process; the first few times have the plastic spill-proof stopper out of the cap to help the flow come out faster.
    - Use the schedule listed in the "Typical Days" section of this book to determine the times to offer the sippy cup.
    - 5 minutes at each meal for about 3-5 days

is all that should be spent trying to 'help them' with the sippy cup if they are not interested.

- o They may seem like they hate it, but they do not hate it and they do **not** hate you. This is just unfamiliar.

- o In addition to mealtimes, keep the sippy cup available throughout the day with water in it, but do not put too much emphasis on it.
- o Here are some little phrases that help you to keep calm: "You can drink from the sippy cup and be great at it." Or, "You are a big boy, and you can drink from the big boy cup. I'm not worried."
- o Do not make the 'stress face.' If a sippy cup shows up while mom makes 'stress face' every time, then they begin to associate sippy cups with...stress.
- o It may take a solid three days before they are really starting to get the hang of it.
- o You will want to turn back. You may even be afraid that the child may dehydrate.
- o They will decrease the overall amount of milk that they drink at this time, and that is normal. Do not let that scare you. If you are worried about growth or development, then contact your pediatrician.
- o You may still offer a sippy cup of whole milk as a part of the nighttime routine. Wipe the teeth down with a thin cloth or brush the teeth prior to bedtime so that the milk residue does not compromise the integrity of the tooth enamel.
- o Stay calm and confident. They will figure this out.

SECTION FOUR: SLEEP

_____

_____

Establishing Healthy Sleep Habits

"If you lie down, you will not be afraid; when you lie down, your sleep will be sweet."
Proverbs 3:24

GETTING YOUR BABY TO SLEEP

"My baby is 10 months old. She cries every night and wakes up 1 or 2 times to feed. I am so exhausted I can hardly think straight."

Now here is the real reason most of you are reading this material! If you follow these directions, you will have a much better chance of enjoying your evenings and nights on into toddlerhood.

As long as this baby is healthy, the following advice—IF FOLLOWED—will produce a much better night's sleep. **These principles are designed to work together and if you change one or leave one out you will not get the expected results.**

This is not another CIO (cry it out) book. We are working with the body's natural rhythm and routines to establish healthy sleep habits that benefit the entire family. Getting 10-12 hours of sleep in a row is essential for normal growth and development, supports the body's immune system, allows the gastrointestinal tract to rest and is the cornerstone of healthy, happy households. In short, this is just normal.

We will always come from a position of encouragement and support. We will not judge or tear down any parent who does not choose our method. There are differing ways of raising children and if you choose another method that is perfectly fine. We want you to be confident in how you have chosen to raise your family and live your lives—day and night—on purpose.

The only thing that we ask is that you parent out of truth and not out of fear.

The basic Moms on Call sleep principles
- o Cribs are the only sleep environment that we recommend. One less than 5 years old with a new mattress, a mattress cover and tight-fitted crib sheet.
- o The baby sleeps in a safe crib in their room. The further away from the smell of the "kitchen of their favorite restaurant" (that's you!) the better they will rest.
- o The crib must be free of any stimulation such as mobiles, toys of any variety, stuffed animals, loose blankets, or light up fish tanks. We like two items in the crib: (1) The baby (2) Thin breathable bumper pad secured around the perimeter. In short, the sleep environment is completely safe and so boring there is nothing to do there but sleep. We want them to associate the crib with sleep, not play.
- o White noise is on all night long and must be loud enough for you to be able to hear clearly from the other side of a closed door. This helps their brains get into the deep, refreshing, REM sleep and stay there longer. Place it approximately two feet from the head of the crib but not in the crib.
- o White noise is only white noise, not lullabies or ocean waves. See the "Products" page of our website for the one we like best, at the best price. www.momsoncall.com
- o At night, the room is pitch-black dark, no night-lights, closet lights or hallway lights. Black out

109

curtains are wonderful. However, there can be some indirect light coming through the windows for **nap**times.

- o Temperature of the house is between 68-72 degrees F.
  - • 68-72 degrees F. - baby is wearing a cotton, short sleeve onesie without any embroidered elements that are scratchy on the inside. Over that, the baby can wear a light cotton, long-sleeve, long pant sleeper with footies.
- o If you do not have control over the temperature in the room.
  - • Cold -64-68 degrees F. - baby can wear a *fleece*, zip-up sleeper with footies.
  - • Hot -if it is 73-78 degrees F -Baby is wearing short sleeve light cotton sleeper or just a onsie.
- o We get into more trouble with babies getting too hot than we do with them getting too cold. Remember, they have brand new effective metabolisms, so they tend to like the room a bit cool. That said, all babies are individuals and it is fine to experiment with the temperature a bit to see what your baby's preferences are.
- o Babies learn by association and routine. Babies will associate bath-time with bedtime, dark-time with bedtime, and white noise with bedtime. We are using the way they learn to help them learn to sleep all night.
- o Once the baby goes in the crib for nighttime, he stays in the crib. That is the place where the atmosphere is conducive to sleep.
- o **Middle of the night feedings** – There should not

be any reason to feed a healthy baby over 6 months old in the middle of the night. If they awaken and cry at night, let them cry until they fall back asleep. In three to five nights, they will not awaken at that time in the night. They will not starve because they miss a feeding at 2 a.m.

o They will increase their daytime feedings incrementally over the course of the next three days and get exactly what they need. So, have an extra ounce or two in each daytime bottle or let them spend 5 more minutes at each breastfeeding.

o Wc tcach thcm what nighttime looks like in our home. Nighttime is time for sleep. It is time to be in their own bedroom.

o We never do sleep training when our children are legitimately sick (teething does not count).

o Follow the schedules listed in the "Typical Days" section of this book. It will keep enough time between supper and bedtime feedings to make sure that they are hungry enough to eat well before that long stretch of sleep.

o Bedtime should start between 7pm and 8pm at the latest.

o Morning begins at 6:30-7:30 am every day **even if we have to wake them**. Starting the day on time is an essential aspect of maintaining healthy sleep habits. We do not let them "make up" for lost sleep. We "transfer" lost sleep to the next scheduled sleep time.

o Do not allow any naps to last longer than 2 -3 hours. Unless they are going to one nap a day; then that nap can last 3-4 hours.

Sleeping: Bedtime Routines –
- o Begins with bath time. They have a bath every night. Water is warm.
- o After the bath, and once the baby is diapered and clothed, we have what we call **'Tender Time'** -dim the lights, read a book, play soft music, sing to your baby. This is the sweetest time of day.
- o Feed very well. Burp (the baby).
- o Never allow your child to go to sleep with milk/formula residue on their gums/teeth. This causes painful tooth decay. That means no bottles in the crib!
- o Place the baby in the crib.
- o Turn on white noise.
- o Make sure the room is completely dark. This way the light does not cause additional stimulation as they are trying to get to sleep.
- o Then **your job is to stay out of the room** until 6:30-7:00 am. Do not engage in any way. Do not talk to them through the door. They can do this!
- o Let the baby cry on and off—even if the crying lasts over an hour or two! They <u>will</u> fall asleep. If you are consistent, after three to five nights they will sleep at bedtime, in their crib, and fall asleep almost immediately— but only if YOU do not go in their room and pick them up. Give it three to five nights. Yes, you can . . . really, we believe in you . . . YOU CAN DO IT!
- o More importantly, *they* can do it. Even when they get to that cry that makes you think; "they cannot settle down," the truth is they **can and they will** if we give them enough time and stay out of the way.
- o Speak the truth to your heart – **They are safe, they are loved and they can learn to do this.**
- o Parents are always so afraid the child will feel

112

abandoned. So we have to ask: are they abandoned? No! No, they are not abandoned. Let's parent out of that truth. They are not abandoned and you will show up every morning at that predictable time and they will be ready for your warm embrace.

o   Somewhere between nights 7 and 10, we will have a bad night or two as the new routine is settling in. This is normal and does not require intervention.

o   Use this routine and do not leave out one step! This has worked for thousands of frustrated families and we are confident that it will be just as effective for you and yours.

o   If you would like your baby to sleep for 10-12 hours in a row, follow these instructions to the letter. And remember to follow these steps for at least three to five nights in a row before you decide for certain if this is working. No cheating!

o   As babies get older, sometimes this process can take up to a week. If you feel that you are in need of additional instruction or support, Moms on Call offers personalized consultations.

o   Right before bed is when we love to read Bible stories and speak of the wonderful promises that God has in store for those who love Him. We will hold the kids and tell them that they are brave and strong, and tell them how proud we are of who they are. It is never too early to begin to speak blessings over your children!

During this 3-5 night transition, babies cry because this is not what happened yesterday and they are creatures of habit. The only way to reset that little internal clock, and teach them the new schedule is to stay consistent for the amount of time it takes for them to learn (typically 3-5 nights). They will begin to learn on night two that you show up every morning on time and by night three they are really beginning to understand the new routine. By night 4 or 5, they are enjoying the nice long stretches of sleep that allow their bodies to relax, repair, and rejuvenate.

SLEEP-TIME TROUBLESHOOTING

6-12 months of age

The consistency of nighttime is such a huge piece of the puzzle and we have that in place. Now, it is a matter of working thru a few details. We will get there.

The top reasons that we are going beyond the 5 nights of fussiness/crying at night:

1. **Missed one of the details of the nighttime plan outlined in the sleep section**. Leaving out one piece of the puzzle can affect the success of nighttime. If you did not like the white noise or feed too often in the evening; we can have wake up times in the night. Review all of the sleep guidelines and make sure that you are following each one. Babies cannot get to sleep too late. Bedtime is ideally around 7:30pm.

2. **They are still working on increasing their intake during the day**.
To ensure that the baby is getting at least 24 ounces per day, offer the baby a bottle supplement with formula or breastmilk for the first and last feedings of the day x 3-4 days. If they are taking over an ounce in the supplement then they need to have additional ounces after those feedings more regularly.

3. **Some babies have a loud 'twilight sleep' stage in the night**. If they are having on and off fussiness in the night, past night 5, this is typically the culprit and it is

115

not something we can change. They are asleep, and you can see on the baby monitor that their eyes are closed. They are just making some loud noise in their sleep. Occasionally the loudness of their own voice fully wakes them up. The key is that they learn how to get themselves back to sleep. This is an important and valuable life skill.

4. **The white noise machines are an essential piece of the puzzle.** Be sure to get one intended for adults so they do not have all those annoying lights. They need to be loud enough for you to hear them from outside the baby's room with the door closed.

5. **If you are having trouble beyond a week** and would like to partner with a Moms on Call trained consultant, we have many options. Look us up at www.momsoncall.com.

6. **For sleeptime troubleshooting beyond 12-13 months -** See the *Moms On Call Toddler Book* for expanded instructions.

So how do you handle resentful friends or neighbors when they find out that your child/children sleep all night? At Moms on Call we are always supportive. Whatever method any parent chooses to put into practice is their choice. We often will say things like.

"If you need to borrow the book, I have it. But if what you are doing is working for you, then that is really great."

MAINTAINING GOOD SLEEP HABITS

"We are at my mom's for vacation and Sterling does not want to sleep. She usually goes to sleep so well. She has just been fussy ever since we got here."

Your child's sleep pattern may be interrupted when:

- o They reach certain developmental milestones - i.e., crawling, walking, language explosion.
- o They change environments or daily routines (vacation, holidays).
- o They are recovering from an illness.
- o When you get rid of the pacifier (see 'Getting Rid of the Pacifier' on the following page)

The trick is to get right back into the healthy routine. It is much easier to *re-establish* great sleep habits. But the longer we put it off, the longer it may take to return to the nice long stretches of sleep.

- o Review the basic sleep principles outlined in the sleep section of this book and in 1-3 nights, you will be right back on track. This is all a part of healthy sleep habits.
- o If you go on vacation and are sharing a room or just have to "keep the peace" no matter what; then return to your great sleep routines once you get home.
- o If your child is suffering from a virus or infection, then it is fine to go in their room at night. Provide whatever comforts they need and when

they feel better, spend the 1-3 nights it will take to get them back on the great sleep routine they enjoyed prior to their illness, 10-12 hours in a row.

Getting Rid of the Pacifier

When?
When YOU are ready. It will take a 3-5 day adjustment complete with a few tantrums and extra crying at naptimes but they can do it!!

Truth: My child can live and thrive without the pacifier. He/She/They can do it!

What to say: (to a child 12 months or older)"You don't need the paci anymore. You will be just fine. Let's play with your blocks (or any other distracting acitivty)."
What to do:
1. Get rid of all the pacis – just throw them away. The child does not watch that happen. Throw them away when the child is asleep.
2. Trust in the truth. (stated above)
3. At naptime they go down for a nap at the same time/environment as usual. The naptime may be difficult for 5-7 days but stay consistent. See naptime instructions in the following section.

NAPTIME

Sleeping: Naptimes

- Room temperature is between 68-72° F
- Allow a little bit of sunlight into the room to help regulate that natural distinction between daytime and nighttime sleep
- White noise is on LOUD and is only white noise, not lullabies or ocean waves. Use white noise for the entire naptime. See the "Products" page of our website for the one we like best www.momsoncall.com
- Try to get at least 2 naps in the crib per day as much as reality allows.
- The goal of naptime is to keep them in the crib until as close to the next *scheduled* feeding time as possible.
- They can occasionally nap in the carseat, stroller or swing as long as they remain properly strapped in and monitored at all times.
- Provide a consistent nap schedule where the naps start at the same time each day. (See the "Typical days" section of this book)
- Your job is to provide the routine and environment and their job is to sleep.
- You may notice that they "wake up" about 30-45 minutes into the nap, this is normal. It is called 'twilight sleep" They will fuss on and off for 15-20 minutes and then get back to sleep. Give them an opportunity to get through this for at least two naps in the day.

- When initiating the nap schedule (for starters), pick two naps a day and they stay in the crib for the same two naps which will **start at the same time** each day. It will take about a week for their little internal clocks to be set. So, stay consistent.
- When they get about 6-8 months old, they get so curious, that we have our good nap days and our bad ones. On the bad nap days, we have to tell ourselves that they can "cry, play, or sleep" but they stay in the crib and have that downtime for at least an hour and fifteen minutes twice a day (at the same times each day) as much as reality allows. Keep the white noise on loud and stay consistent even when the baby is not.
- At any time that you feel that you need extra support, contact us at www.momsoncall.com to set up a personal consultation.

6 -12 months
- Two good naps a day are sufficient
- The morning should be a minimum of one hour and a maximum of two hours (from the start of the naptime, not from the start of the time that they actually fell asleep)
- The afternoon nap is 1 ½ hour minimum to 2 hours maximum (from the start of the naptime, not from the start of the time that they actually fell asleep) AND must be over by 4pm.

12-15 months
- The 6-12 month nap principles (above) apply until they are ready to go to one nap a day.
- When are they ready? If they are having more bad nap days than good ones for 2 weeks.

DROPPING THE MORNING NAP

12-15 months

These guidelines are for early toddlers that are getting 10-12 hours of nighttime sleep in a row. (If they are not, then read the nighttime sleep section and do that first)

- o We will go to one nap typically between 12-15 months.
- o We go to one nap when the child is having more bad nap days than good ones for 2 weeks given that you are using the other Moms on Call guidelines.
- o Typically the afternoon nap gets really unpredictable.
- o The adjustment to one nap will take a week
- o Pick a start time between 12-1:30pm. Whatever time you choose is the time that the nap starts every day.
- o The one nap is a minimum of 1½ hours long and a maximum of 3 hours long (from the start of the naptime, not the start of the time that they fell asleep) It most definitely needs to be over by 4pm.
- o The nap is 'cry, play or sleep'. If they do mostly crying, they can get up after an hour and a half but keep them awake until nighttime. Then, start naptime at the same time the next day. They will start to sleep more when we keep the nap**TIMES** consistent (i.e. 12:30-2:30 every day).
- o If they did not fall asleep right away, the naptime is still over 3 hours from the time the nap started (not the time they fell asleep). Which means, you

may have to wake them up from their nap.

- o We will not ruin everything by having a weekend getaway or staying at the zoo too long; as long as we keep the same nap schedule in place when reality allows.
- o If we are doing so much running around each day that we cannot establish a regular naptime, they will be cranky and will have a harder time adjusting to the daily routines. It does not make you a bad mom; it is a trade-off. In reality, some of us have unpredictable schedules for various reasons. Go with it.
- o Naptimes are more successful when nighttime sleep of 10-12 hours in a row is firmly established.
- o The hardest part of the transition is keeping them awake until that one naptime for the first week.
- o To keep them awake- change environments, use distraction, and work at it.
- o If they do not have a good nap, keep nighttime solid. They do not get to "go to bed early". Even though they are cranky in the evening, we want to set the inner 24-hour clock by keeping times consistent. If they "go to bed early" we risk throwing off the next day's naptime success.

TRANSFERRING TO A TODDLER BED

One of the biggest questions that we receive is "When is my child ready to move into a toddler bed?"
We move to a toddler bed as soon as they either can climb out of the crib, we need the crib for baby #2, or they reach their third birthday, whichever comes first. Each child is different, so there is not a specific age when all kids come out of the crib and into a toddler bed but sometime before the third birthday will be fine. Let's first establish that you love your child and will be reinforcing your child with positive statements such as:

- o "You can do this."
- o "I believe in you."
- o "You are so brave."
- o "I love you enough to want you to learn to sleep like a big kid."
- o "God has not given us a spirit of fear but of power, love and a sound mind."

A few ground rules:

- o Step one: **Believe that your child can sleep in a toddler bed, in their room, all night and be great at it!**
- o We show our toddlers what nighttime looks like. They will test their new freedom. If we allow them to come out of the room, keep us *in* the room or engage them in

conversation after we say good night—then *that* is their new norm.

- They do not need to talk to you, go potty, have a drink of water, or come out of their room. Nighttime is the time to stay in their room and they will be great at it, given about a week to adjust.
- After that door closes we have a strict "no engagement" policy. They are cute and resourceful, so be strong.
- Put the ideal nighttime atmosphere in place right from the start. Those first three nights that your toddler goes into their toddler bed is crucial.
- Do not allow any naps to last longer than 2 hours. If they are going to take one nap a day, then that nap can last 3 hours.
- Naptime should be over by 4 p.m. If the naps are too long or go too late they can affect nighttime sleep.
- **Middle of the night feedings –** There should not be any reason to feed a healthy toddler in the middle of the night. They will not starve because they miss a feeding at 2 a.m.! They will cry for a few nights because things have changed (not because they are starving.)
- **The adult white noise machines are an essential piece of the puzzle.** Be sure to get one intended for adults so they do not have all

those annoying lights. They need to be loud enough for you to hear them from outside the toddler's room with the door closed. We have a link to the one we like best on the products page of our website www.momsoncall.com. This noise helps to lull the brain into that restorative and restful REM sleep that is so essential to growth and development.

o   If your toddler needs it, a night-light is fine. Our favorite is the Good Nite Lite (www.goodnitelite.com). You can set the "sun to come up" at any specific morning time that suits your family schedule (7 am is ideal).

o   We do not sleep train when our child is legitimately sick. If it happens in the middle of sleep training, then we stop and restart once they are feeling better.

o   The temperature of the room should be between 68-72 degrees F.

o   The child's room is child-proofed – completely. Here are some things to look out for but this is not an exhaustive list. **This step is crucial.** Outlets are covered (even ones with things plugged into them), there are not heavy objects like televisions on top of dressers that could fall on top of a child, the blind cords are cut so nothing is dangling and could be a strangulation hazard, all ingestible items such as medication, diaper cream and shampoo are locked away and not just in a drawer amongst other things.

- If there is a door in their room that leads to a bathroom, it is closed and locked restricting any access that a toddler has to a bathroom with running water or other dangers. (An eye-hook latch at adult eye-level is great for this.)
- **The doorknob on the bedroom door is switched so it locks from the outside/hallway side.** Just like the crib restricted access to the room, the closed/locked door restricts access to the entire house.

Locked Door (expanded)
This is simply a safety measure so that the toddler does not have access to an entire house filled with dangers in the middle of the night when parents are sleeping. It is too dangerous.

If there is a fire, an adult or firefighter will have to get them out of the house, and toddlers like to hide when they are scared. We don't want to have to search a 3,000 square foot home, we want to be able to find them in a 10X10 foot room and know exactly where they are.
We NEVER mention that scenario to our toddlers.

We simply tell them that we close the door to keep them safe.

This is also important so that we can help them learn that their room is a safe and appropriate place for sleeping all night.
For those of you who have just been waiting for permission to close that door, you have it. Close it and lock it from the hallway side to keep that child safe.

Sleep Training Routine
The first night that your child transitions to the new bed, have your routine ready.
  o Give the child/children a bath.
  o Dress the child in their pajamas while playing soft music and dim the lights.
  o Read them a book (two maximum; have them picked out already). At the end of book #2, make a positive statement such as "Okay, it's time for bed and I am going to be in the living room and you are going to stay in this bed like a big kid and fall asleep. You are so good and brave and I can't wait to see you in the morning." Or ""This is your new bed. You are going to be great at sleeping right here all night long. I love you, I believe in you and I will see you when the sun comes up." Do not linger.
  o Be ready! This statement may induce a crying fit or a barrage of manipulation. The child may try to talk you out of leaving the room, or try to follow you out of the room. We must get out anyways.
  o We leave and **close the door**.
  o Once that door is closed it does not open until it is time to start the next day. It opens when the sun comes up just like you said it would.
  o Our job is to stay out and not to engage in any

conversation. We will not be addressing any behaviors, commenting on any requests or going back in the room, lest we fear for their lives.

- o **Stay out and do not engage in conversation or direction of any type**. That is our entire job at night. It is the hardest thing you have ever had to do thus far. But we will tell our hearts the truth.

The truth is:
They are safe
They are loved
They can learn to do this

- o Even if your child is screaming on the other side, remember that in 3-7 days this child will learn how to sleep in his/her own bed. We are establishing a routine that will help your child have greater contentment and confidence in the long run.
- o Again, do not sit outside the door, listening to the crying and crying yourself. You are not a horrible parent. (This is harder for us than it is for them, although it may not sound like it at first!)
- o At this age, it usually only takes about 3 days but can take up to a week if we engage them after we close that door.
- o THIS IS CRUCIAL! The next morning, we start the day at the same wake-up time (7 am), even if we have to wake them up.
- o Have support. If mom and dad are living in the same home, make sure that you are both

in agreement and can support each other. This will help immensely. Help each other.

o   Be consistent. If you plan for this and do it the first three to five nights, the rest of your child's toddlerhood nights will be much easier.

A few more tips

<u>Are you afraid they will wake up a sibling?</u>
We never "save" the quiet one. Siblings have an innate ability to sleep through loudness. But if another child wakes, they can get themselves back to sleep without our help and will do so better without us in the room offering up extra stimulation in the middle of the night.

We just let them work it out. First they learn how to accommodate their siblings then they learn how to accommodate classmates, then others in the community and so on. It is a natural part of life and remember, we are not in the business of conflict avoidance but life-preparedness. (Laura – I child-proofed the twins' room and when I put them to bed, I closed the door and let them cry it out for three nights. And let me tell you, they put on a show of tears and banging on the door, but I persevered. Now they are wonderful sleepers.)

<u>Night one can be trying.</u> They may kick the door, cry, scream, throw things out of their dresser drawers, pull off their pull-up/diaper and paint the walls with poop. Remember, IF YOU WANT A BEHAVIOR TO CONTINUE, PAY ATTENTION TO IT. If you want them to do any of those things again, then go back in the room. It will continue night after night. If you do **not** want any of

129

those behaviors to continue, then stay out, go to bed and open the door when the sun comes up just like you said. We will address any unwanted nighttime behavior – in the morning.

The morning is important. When we open that door in the morning, we have our "confident face" on. That is when we address any antics that went on the night before such as . . .

- o "You did not need to sleep here in front of the door when you could have slept in that comfy bed all night, Oh, well, you'll get the hang of it, let's start our day"
- o "You didn't have to pull all your clothes out of your drawers last night when you'd be great at snuggling up in your bed and sleeping there all night. Oh, well, we'll get these picked up and start our day" – smile and confidence
- o "You didn't have to throw your pull-up/diaper in the corner. It stays on all night. Oh, well we'll throw this one out and you can have a fresh one at naptime. Let's start our day"

Anything that went on in that room the night before meets our completely unconcerned confident face and we make a clear statement and move on. They can do this, that is our motto and we will stick to it.

Our confidence will be contagious.
This method is intent on encouraging you to support your toddler as they adjust to healthy nighttime habits that will help them to be physically healthy, and equip them to enjoy life because they are no longer exhausted and over-stimulated (and neither are you). They need long stretches of sleep just like we do. One week of hard
130

work and you can look forward to evening time, decrease the unhealthy levels of stress in the household, get full nights of restful sleep and maybe even have a chance to have time in the evening with your spouse and remember why you made babies.

If we go in and some of us might, then it takes longer but it can still be done. There is no point of no return. Regroup, reread the sleep section of the book and start fresh the next night. You can do it!!

Need help, support or to ask a few questions? Contact us at www.momsoncall.com for more information about our personalized consultations.

SECTION FIVE: TYPICAL DAYS

_____

_____

Enjoying The Routine Of Family Life

"There is an appointed time for everything. And there is a time for every event under heaven."
Ecclesiastes 3:1

TYPICAL DAYS

"I just want to know what kind of schedule my baby should be on. I feel so lost."

The following schedules are guidelines. Any of the following schedules can be moved in their entirety ½ hour earlier or later to adjust to your personal home schedule.

We understand that schedules these days need to be flexible. We also know that the babies and toddlers who have regular nap times and feeding times tend to be more content. There is a delicate balance between being so scheduled that you cannot enjoy life and being so flexible that you cannot enjoy your family.

This is a gradual process and not black and white. We do not want to overwhelm you with details. If one schedule is working for you and you are not ready to progress to the next, then stay with that one as long as it is working.

When you see a "/" between two times listed in the schedules that means you can start anytime between those two times.

Morning naps should continue as long as you can possibly get them to take one! Usually they will go down to one nap around 15 months. (See nap section for details.)

TYPICAL DAY 4-6 MONTHS

*(The **bottle contains 6-8 ounces** and the sippy cup will contain 2-4 ounces of breastmilk or formula unless otherwise noted. Baby food amounts do not really matter; we show amounts because parents want an idea of what is typical.)*

7 am   Wakes up; drinks formula/breastmilk

8 am   ½ jar fruit with 1-2 tablespoons of baby cereal. May begin to try sippy cup just for familiarity

9 am   Naptime 1-1 ½ hours

11 am   Formula/breastmilk

12pm   2-4 oz. veggies, 2-4 oz. fruit with 1-2 tablespoons of baby cereal – May begin to give sippy cup

12:30/1:30   Nap (1 ½ - 2 hours) -pick one time between 12:30 and 1:30 and start nap at that time each day

3:00 pm   Breastmilk/formula

4:00 pm   2-4 oz. veggies, 2-4 oz. of fruit with a sippy cup of formula/breastmilk

5:00 pm   Make take a small catnap

6:00 pm   Keep awake from now until bathtime/bedtime (do 10 min. of tummy time – release that energy!)

6:30 pm   Start bath time routine

7:00 pm   Breastfeed or bottle feed

7:30 pm   In the crib for the night (see "Sleep" Section)

TYPICAL DAY 6-8 MONTHS
(Sippy cup keeps showing up)

7am	Bottle or nurse (6-8 oz.)
8am	Baby food and a sippy cup*
9am	Start nap (ideally 1 ½ hour)
11am	Bottle or nurse (6-8 oz.)
Noon	Baby food and a sippy cup*
12:30/1:30	Nap (ideally 1 ½-2 hours)-pick one time between 12:30 and 1:30 and start nap at that time each day
3pm	Bottle or nurse (6-8 oz.)
4/5pm	Anytime between 4 and 5 pm baby food and a sippy cup* available
5:00pm	Catnap – no longer than 30 min if they still take one
6:30	Bath
7pm	Last nighttime feeding (6-8 oz.) bottle or nurse
7:30pm	In crib for the night (See "Sleep" Section for additional instructions)

*Sippy cups have 2-4 ounces of formula/breastmilk

136

TYPICAL DAY 8-10 MONTHS
(Add snacks and finger foods)

7am	Bottle or nurse (6-8 oz.)
8am	Breakfast -Baby foods, finger foods, sippy cup*
9am	Nap 1-1 ½ hours
10:30	Snack of finger foods and a sippy cup*
11am	Bottle or nurse here (6-8 oz.)
Noon	Lunch -Baby food, finger foods, sippy*
12:30-1:30pm	Nap (ideally 1 ½-2 hours)-pick one time between 12:30 and 1:30 and start nap at that time each day
2:30/3pm	Snack of finger foods and a sippy cup*
3:00pm	Bottle or nurse (6-8 oz.)
5pm	Supper -Baby foods, finger foods, sippy cup*
6:30	Bath
7pm	Last nighttime feed (6-8 oz) bottle or nurse
7:30pm	In crib for the night (See "Sleep" Section for additional instructions)

*Sippy cups have 2-4 ounces of formula/breastmilk

137

TYPICAL DAY 11 MONTHS
*(**Three meals a day**)*

7am	Bottle or Nurse (6-8oz.)
8am	Breakfast -Baby foods, finger foods, sippy cup*
9am	Nap (1-1 ½ hours)
10:30/11am	Snack with sippy cup*
Noon	Lunch -Baby foods, finger foods, sippy cup*
12:30/1:30pm	Nap (ideally 1 ½-2 hours)-pick one time between 12:30 and 1:30 and start nap at that time each day
3/3:30pm	Snack with sippy cup*
5/6pm	Supper -Baby foods, finger foods, sippy cup*
6:30pm	Bath
7pm	Last nighttime feeding (6-8 oz.) bottle or nurse
7:30pm	In crib for the night (See "Sleep" section for additional instructions)

* Sippy cups have 2-4 oz of formula/breastmilk. Having dropped 2 bottles, they will eat more and take more out of the sippy cup in preparation for the 12-month independent feeding stage. They will get what they need.

TYPICAL DAY 12-15 MONTHS
(Three meals and **two naps** per day schedule)

7am	Sippy cup
8am	**Breakfast***
9am	Nap (ideally for 1- 1 ½ hrs)
10:30am	Sippy cup and a snack
Noon	**Lunch***
12:30/1:30pm	Nap (ideally 1 ½ - 2hours)- pick one time between 12:30 and 1:30 and start nap at that time each day
3/3:30pm	Sippy cup and a snack
5/6 pm	**Supper*-** Sometime between 5pm and 6 pm have family supper
6:30pm	Bath
7pm	Sippy cup while you read them a book
7:30pm	In crib for the night (See "Sleep" Section)

*Mealtimes are pea-sized, mushable versions of what you are having plus a sippy cup of whole milk (avoid low-fat meals for toddlers- they need healthy fats.)

*Sippy cups have 2-6 ounces of whole milk and there are <u>no more bottles</u> (see weaning section for more info.)

Morning naps should continue as long as you can possibly get them to take one! (see nap section for details)

TYPICAL DAY 12-15 MONTHS
(Three meals and **one nap** per day schedule)

7am	Door opens, start of day, sippy cup
8am	**Breakfast***
9:00am	Playtime – work at keeping them awake
10am	Sippy cup and a snack
11:30am	**Lunch***
12/1:00pm	Nap- pick one time between 12:00 and 1:00 and start nap at that time each day (ideally 2- 3 hours)
3:30/4pm	Sippy cup and a snack
5/6 pm	**Supper*** -Sometime between 5pm and 6 pm have family supper
6:30pm	Bath
7/7:30pm	Bedtime (see SLEEP section)

*Mealtimes are pea-sized, mushable versions of what you are having plus a sippy cup of whole milk (avoid low-fat meals for toddlers- they need healthy fats)

*Sippy cups have 2-6 ounces of whole milk and there are <u>no more bottles</u> (see weaning section for more info.)

SECTION SIX: SAFETY

Ways To Keep Your Baby Safe

"I will lift my eyes to the hills - from whence comes my help? My help comes from the Lord, who made heaven and earth.
Psalm 121:1-2

IMMUNIZATIONS

"Can I give my baby Acetaminophen before his immunizations to help it not hurt as much?"

Acetaminophen will not take away the pain of the actual injection. As a matter of fact, the baby will have forgotten the incident by the time you walk out the door. (It will probably take *you* much longer to forget.) We all get through it. We hate it, but we do get through it.

Site
- o   Given in thighs or arms
- o   May be red and/or swollen for 2-3 days at site of injections
- o   May have small pea-sized knots for several weeks after discoloration resolves

Fever
- o   Fever 101°F up to 103.5°F rectally is expected for up to 24 hours after the immunizations are given (with the exception of the 12 month immunizations)
- o   Acetaminophen may be given every 4 hours according to the baby's weight – see your pediatrician's handout or website

When to seek medical care
- o   Temp over 103.5°F rectally
- o   Temp over 101.5°F for more than 24 hours after the immunizations were administered

- Crying inconsolably for 2 hours
- Seizure activity (uncontrollable shaking)
- Signs of allergic reaction (very rare) generally will happen within the first 15-20 minutes after administration of immunizations.
  - Difficulty breathing
  - Wheezing
  - Hives
  - Pale and clammy
  - Difficulty swallowing

Moms on Call LLC is in favor of vaccinating children. It is what the American Academy of Pediatrics recommends. Although the MMR (Measles Mumps and Rubella) vaccine is not administered until one year of age, you may have heard about studies linking the MMR vaccine with autism. This study has been completely debunked and retracted. More information is available at cdc.gov.

This much we **do** know. Prior to the MMR vaccination, over 100,000 children a year died of these combined diseases. If your child does not get immunized and contracts one of these diseases, it puts them and other children at risk, especially children under one year who have not yet been vaccinated.

The types of vaccinations that your child will get at 2, 4 and 6 months generally include:
- DTP (Tetanus Diptheria Pertussis)
- IPV (Injectable Polio Vaccine)
- Prevnar (Protects against a bacteria that can cause meningitis and pneumonia)
- HIB (Haemophilus B Influenzae - another bacteria that can cause meningitis)
- Hep B (Hepatitis B - a disease of the liver

transmitted through the blood and body fluids of infected carriers)

Some of these immunizations are combined in one shot, so the most your child should get at one time is four shots; two in one thigh, two in the other. It is over very quickly.

After immunizations the baby is generally a little sleepier for 3-4 hours, then possibly fussy for the next 4-6. You can take the Band-Aids® off after about an hour. If the baby is fussy or develops a fever, use Acetaminophen every four hours as needed as directed by your Pediatrician.

> **Note**: In the summertime, especially when baby's legs are exposed, they may try to pull off the Band-Aid® and eat it. Watch carefully!

12-15 month vaccinations generally include:
  o Varivax (Chicken Pox vaccine)—if your child has not had the actual chicken pox yet
  o MMR (Measles, Mumps, and Rubella) Three diseases with rash and/or cough. Any of these diseases can be fatal.
  o These shots can go in the fatty tissue behind the arm or the fatty tissue in the thighs.

The 12-month vaccinations have side effects that are different from other immunizations. The **MMR** can cause a fever of up to 102.5°F rectally from 7-14 days after the immunization was given. It can also produce a pink pin-prickly rash that blanches with pressure on the torso and face. If your baby experiences these

144

symptoms, call your pediatrician and remind them that your baby had immunizations 1-2 weeks ago. These side effects are not dangerous and resolve on their own in about 48 hours from the time they began. The baby is also generally playful and alert throughout the extent of the symptoms.

The **Varivax** vaccine can produce a rash that looks like small pus-filled bumps that generally starts on the abdomen. These bumps are only contagious 20% of the time and only to people who have not had chicken pox and only if they were exposed to the pus inside the bumps. This rash should also resolve on its own in 4-5 days.

15-18 month vaccinations generally include:
- o   DTP (Tetanus, Diptheria, Pertussis)
- o   IPV (Injectable Polio Vaccine)
- o   HIB (Haemophilus B Influenzae - another bacteria that can cause meningitis)
- o   Possibly Prevnar (which protects against a bacteria that can cause meningitis and pneumonia)

CHILDPROOFING/SAFETY

Childproofing: Accidents are just that—ACCIDENTS. However, there are measures that we can take to minimize our child's risk. According to the American Heart Association, injuries are the leading cause of death in children and young adults. Childproofing and being knowledgeable about possible hazards can help you minimize that risk for your child.

We cannot stress enough the importance of taking regular CPR training. The question you should ask yourself and your child's caretakers is not only, "When did you take your last CPR class?" but more importantly, "If my child were choking or unresponsive, would I know what to do?" (Yes, we know that you said "Call 911" in your head, but there are life saving steps that you can take while 911 is on the way!)

Please, please, please, know what to do if your child is choking. CPR classes are offered through the American Heart Association and the Red Cross. Almost all area hospitals offer regular classes.

Common Safety Issues. Here is a quick but not exhaustive checklist for some common safety issues.

o   Put plastic guards on all sharp corners.
o   Put outlet protectors for outlets not being used and an outlet cover attachment that can be used on outlets that *are* being used. Children will try to play with cords that are plugged in.
o   Keep blind cords short and out of reach of children.
o   Put safety latches on all cabinets and drawers.
o   Move all cleaning supplies from under the sink and put in a high cabinet that locks.
o   Put plastic doorknob covers on doors and a hook-eye latch on any doors leading to basements or stairs.
o   Keep a set of keys to all doors in case your child locks themselves in a room.
o   Keep all plastic bags out of reach - including dry cleaner bags and grocery bags.
o   Install infant gates at top and bottom of stairs. Do not use pressure-mounted gates; use hardware mounted.
o   Never allow your child to play with latex balloons. They generally like to bite them and they can inhale a piece of latex and choke or suffocate. No balloons in the car.
o   Check the safety of the crib. Slats should be no wider than 2 3/8 inches apart. There should be no more than 2 inches between the mattress edges and the crib.
o   Do not put any pillows, stuffed animals or anything in the bed. If you think your child needs more warmth, use a sleeper (fleece zip-up).

Bathroom
- o Keep all medicines in a locked cabinet and out of baby's reach. This means no bottles of vitamins or Ibuprofen on the counter, even with "childproof" caps.
- o Keep shampoo and soap out of reach.
- o Always unplug any appliances to avoid electric shock.
- o Set hot water heater to 120 degrees Fahrenheit. Always check temperature of water before placing child in it.
- o Be aware of what you put in the trash, i.e., pills or razor blades. These items should be put in a trashcan out of child's reach.
- o Put toilet locks on all toilets. I know dad does not like this but children are fascinated with the toilet and can fall in. They also like to flush items down the toilet and dad will not like having to pull the items from the toilet or taking the toilet apart to extract the large clump of Play-Doh®. (Thanks, Patrick and Blake—Laura.)
- o Always empty water out of the bathtub immediately after using it.
- o Put non-skid bath mats on bottom of tub.
- o NEVER LEAVE YOUR CHILD UNATTENDED IN THE BATH FOR ANY REASON FOR ANY LENGTH OF TIME! This means if the phone rings, let it ring! They can leave a message.

Kitchen
- o Always turn pot and pan handles to the back of the stove and cook on back burners.
- o Avoid tablecloths. They can be pulled down with hot food sliding onto baby's head. (As a child, Laura pulled a tablecloth and a pot of hot grits

fell on her foot. The burn marks are still there.)
- Keep all appliances out of reach.
- Place covers on stove controls and a lock on the refrigerator. (They sell these in all colors so they match your kitchen décor.)
- Always be aware of where your child is when transporting hot foods or liquids.
- HOUSE RULE: NO toys on the kitchen floor. You can trip and drop hot liquid on kids.
- Keep aluminum foil and Saran Wrap® out of reach.
- Make sure the stove is anchored to the wall. Make sure all knives and cutlery are out of reach. Sometimes latches on a drawer are not quite enough.
- Never keep kid snack food near any medications, vitamins, or cleaners. (They learn where the snack food is and that is the cabinet they try to get into when you are not looking.)

Living Area
- Be aware of windows. These should have safety locks so they can only be opened a few inches. (May be purchased at home improvement stores.)
- Check all furniture to see if it falls over easily, especially bookcases. Where *we* see a bookcase, a little boy sees a ladder. Anchor your bookcases to the wall. (Trust me, Bryce loved to try this—Jennifer).
- Keep electrical cords out of reach. TV cord can be pulled and cause the TV to come crashing down on a child's head.
- Never leave your child alone with pets.
- Always check stair railing for sturdiness.

Choking

Liquid that is swallowed at meals will usually clear itself in 10-30 seconds.

Solids:
- o If the child is coughing vigorously and can talk and breathe, then do nothing. Do not slap a child on the back who may be choking when they are in the upright position. This can lodge the foreign object in the throat.
- o Removal of a foreign object is best learned in a CPR class.
- o Do not put your fingers in the child's mouth unless you see an object. Only then can you perform a finger sweep of the mouth.

Car Seats

o It is best to have your car seat checked by a professional. Some local fire departments will also check your installation; call first to see which location near you does so.

o Your car seat will come with weight limits. Check the side and back for information on placement and weight requirements.

o Check with your state's department of motor vehicles to get current guidelines.

o Straps need to be snug. The front clip should be at the nipple line and no more than two of your fingers should fit between the strap and your child. Again, note the manufacturer's guidelines. If you have any questions, see a checkpoint near you.

o When tightening the seat in the car, put your knee in the base of the car seat. Then thread the seatbelt through the car seat according to manufacturer's guidelines. The seat should move no more than ½ inch from side to side. Always remember to use the additional safety clip (often sold separately) to clip to the seatbelt.

o The safest place to put a car seat is in the middle of the back seat. If you have two children, the one who requires more of your attention should not be directly behind you, they should be in the backseat, passenger side. Never put a child under 12 years old in the front seat of a car with an airbag. The airbag can deploy with such force that it instantly kills a child. **Never put the car seat in the front seat of a car.**

o Many newer model cars come with a tether attachment. Tether equipment can also be purchased at most baby stores.

QUICK-GRAB FIRST AID KIT

"We are out of town and I think my baby has a fever but we forgot to bring a thermometer."

You will need the following items when you least expect it. Keep one in the car and one at home. These are to be kept out of the reach of children. We recommend buying a container with a handle and a lid. On the inside of the lid, list the pediatrician's number, emergency numbers and the number of Poison Control.

- o Band-Aids®
- o Children's Acetaminophen
- o Children's Ibuprofen
- o Diphenhydramine
- o Digital thermometer
- o Hydrocortisone 0.5%
- o Polysporin®
- o Anti-bacterial wash
- o Hydrogen peroxide
- o Pack of 4x4 Gauze and 2x2 Gauze
- o Ace Bandage
- o Squeezable ice pack
- o Tweezers
- o Medical tape

POISONING

POISON CONTROL
404-616-9000 (Atlanta area)
1-800-222-1222 (other areas)

Always call your poison control center immediately if you think your child has swallowed a poison or other substance, such as medicine, that they should not have had.

You will be asked the following:
- o   What was swallowed?
- o   How much? Always estimate the maximum amount.
- o   How long ago was it swallowed?
- o   What symptoms, if any, is the child showing now?
- o   Age and approximate weight of child. Keep in mind that dads do not always get to go to visits to the pediatrician, and may not know what the child weighs. Post the child's most recent weight on your refrigerator.

Prevention
- o   Keep all chemicals, medicines, and cleaners out of reach and locked!
- o   Get a list from from your local garden center or plant supplier of any poisonous house or outdoor plants. For example, holly berries are poisonous. Get rid of all poisonous houseplants.
- o   Keep alcoholic beverages out of reach and locked.

CLOSING REMARKS

In the Moms on Call logo, you will find the words: Sleep, Feed, Laugh and Love. We want to talk about leading a balanced life filled with moments of sheer laughter and enjoyment. The entire purpose of this resource is to provide you with more time to actually enjoy your children.

Sleep
Families who enjoy healthy sleep habits are happy, content and have a stable foundation in which to handle the regular day-to-day challenges of life (not to mention drive a car without being bleary eyed!).
All of the sleep instructions have a goal in mind. To transform stressed, sleep deprived families that are hanging on for dear life into well-rested, confident people who look forward to daytime *and* nighttime.

We want you to be clear-minded when you are singing to your child before bed, playing with them or reading books, among other things. We even want you to keep your cool when the realities of life hit, finding you trying to dislodge play-doh from the toilet or getting that bubble gum out of your daughter's beautiful curly locks. Setting up a household on a foundation of good rest is what we do and we can't wait for you to enjoy regular nights of sleep.

Feed

The dinner table is a time of togetherness and sharing. We seek to take the stress out of this natural and normal part of life. If there is a perfect time to laugh and play together, then mealtime is one of our favorites. Instead of being so caught up in the number of bites, we would love to have a low-key environment that invites conversation and the occasional use of the pretzels as alien antennae. Fun! Fun! Fun! Kids who enjoy and are involved in mealtimes are much better eaters. Don't force it; let mealtime evolve from stress-ridden battles to your favorite time of day, simply by following the guides that are provided for you in this resource.
If you do not know how to get from here to there, we have taken all the guesswork out for you.

Laugh

A healthy family life involves a good deal of laughter. We need time to play with our children that is not "educational" time or "instructional" time. Just dance, sing and enjoy being together. Freedom! Leave the stress of the workday behind and make a mess, play in the yard, have some hide-and-seek time or break out the tickle monster. We focus on household order so that we can take a break from the activities of daily life, slow down the hustle and bustle and just enjoy the intense blessing and laughter that children bring.

Love

We assume that you are reading this resource because you love your children and desire to really enjoy them. Love comes in many forms. Love means that we will take on the uncomfortable decisions that we have to make in order to provide a clear structure for the household where our children live and thrive. Peppered throughout this resource, we have an overriding theme of support. Love means believing in our children's ability to do the things that life requires. It is at the core of everything that we recommend. So that families can make order out of chaos and love being together again.

At Moms on Call we hope that this resource has been a blessing to your household, given you greater confidence and ultimately helped you to have more time to enjoy life with your precious little ones.

Check out our entire series of books at www.momsoncall.com

The Moms on Call Series

- *Moms on Call Basic Baby Care: 0-6 months*

- *Moms on Call Next Steps Baby Care: 6-15 months*

- *Moms on Call Toddler Book: 15 months to 4 years*

- *Moms on Call scheduler App*

- *Online classes*

- *Instructional videos*

- *Moms on Call Baby Food Introduction Calendar (free download)*